Rebirth
of an
Ancient
Irish Clan

Terence Kearey

MEREO

Mereo Books

2nd Floor, 6-8 Dyer Street, Cirencester, Gloucestershire, GL7 2PF
An imprint of Memoirs Books. www.mereobooks.com
and www.memoirsbooks.co.uk

The Rebirth of an Ancient Clan
ISBN: 978-1-86151-689-3

First published in Great Britain in 2023
by Mereo Books, an imprint of Memoirs Books.

The address for Memoirs Books can be
found at www.mereobooks.com

Mereo Books Ltd. Reg. No. 12157152

Typeset in 10.5/17pt Times
by Wiltshire Associates.
Printed and bound in Great Britain

A Dedication to the Reader in Ogham, the ancient Irish Linear Writing.

BENDACHT FOR CECH N-OEN LEGFAS

'A blessing on all who shall read this'

Ogham inscriptions are usually memorial and read along the edge of the stone from the bottom upwards. The drawing is an artist's impression of how such an inscription might appear on a stone which has been broken.

Contents

LIST OF ILLUSTRATIONS

King of Cairbre, or tribal chief (Toisech), of (Carbury) north-west County Kildare 11th century

Map of Ireland, c 1500

Terence Kearey Coat of Arms, Crest and motto.

T. Kearey RM, Corporal of the gangway HMS Illustrious, 1953.

Introduction

It is important, before I start this family history, to say something about my two great difficulties: one is translating Irish, and the other having an odd initial letter to my name. Both have proved stumbling-blocks, and I will explain. At the time Christ was born (5 BC) the Celts had no written accounts, developing their written word in the eighth century, The Annals of Tigernach (Tigernach hua Braein, Abbot of Clonmacnoise d1088) 1st fragment 374-419 (B.C. – A.D. 150). Their social history appeared, slowly originating from the Christian-Roman world. Constantine accepted Christianity in 313 AD and by 391 AD it was illegal to worship other gods.

J. P. Mallory writes: "Ireland (Scotia), also known as Hibernia, is an island next to Britannia, narrower in its expanse of land but more fertile in its site. It extends from southwest to north. Its near parts stretch towards Iberia (Hiberia) and the Cantabrian Ocean (i.e. the Bay of Biscay), whence it is called Hibernia but is also called Scotia, because it has been colonised by the Scoti."

The book 'The Ancient and Present State of the County and City of Cork' by Charles Smith M.D. tells us that in 125 AD a memorable battle was fought at Ard – Neimheidh, i.e., the 'Great Island,' between Niadh Nuaget and Aengus, monarch of Ireland - recovered the crown of Munster from the latter (Keating, p.227).

The oldest names for the island and its people date from the seventh century (7 AD). The name of Ireland is Scandinavian and today's official name is Eire. The alphabet omits some English letters, one being the letter K. However, today English is a national language of equal standing and highly necessary for worldwide communication, scientific advances, industrialization, internationalism, technology and writing this book.

The first time the name Ciardha (Kearey) is mentioned in the Annals is 992 (Mael-Ruanaig, grandson of Ciarda, king of Cairbre, was killed by the men of Teffa (Loughrea).

The title and subject of this work concern the Kearey 'clan,' a Gaelic word which means 'family', ie sharing a common surname; it originated in Ireland in the 17th century about the time of Cromwell. In ancient times the origins usually were based on one chief. Clan can also mean a tribe, meaning family, stock, and offspring, taken from Latin planta.

It is recorded that the original clan Ciardha later disappeared from history. That I cannot believe, as it suggests that no persons with suitable DNA are now alive, which is almost an impossibility. It is however likely that clan members in troubled times, holding onto family traditions, were sensibly keeping a low profile and living in less populated parts of south western Ireland out of harm's way.

When much of Ireland was taken over by the Anglo-Normans,

clan members changed the spelling of their surname from the Gaelic Ciardha to the Irish/English Ceary, or English, Kearey. That did not change the pronunciation of the name, but it must have helped to achieve neighbourliness, with a home and a job to feed the children. "Surnames did not come into use until the 12th century, at a time when the English language established itself," according to Mallory.

Fortunately *Medieval Ireland* by Michael Richter is a valuable source of information regarding the dynasties which eclipsed the previous tribal kingship groups of the clan, (derbfine, tarfine, indfine) – fixing the community. Previously the clan or sub-clan lived within a mound-surrounded settlement. The society acted and performed in the most basic fashion of life, their homes, lifestyle and community structure no different from any other groups of people throughout the world. It is the influx of other people's different behaviour which generates change and advancement.

After Christianity had been recognised and adopted, the settlement included a church. There were neither towns nor village in ancient Ireland, though watermills were introduced in the seventh century. Family surnames became common from the eleventh century, and this determined the political and cultural landscape of Ireland into the Middle-Ages.

The course of Irish history changed again as the ruling bodies asserted themselves, forcing out the original population through a system of tithes, rents and taxes. This continued by design, greed and ignorance throughout the following centuries; the monied classes and landed gentry disregarded the working peasantry, who had a right to life and expectation. Strife and sorrow became the result, caused by ignorance and selfishness. A lack of farsightedness reigned, which gave nobody any permanent satisfaction.

In 1166 Mac Murrough, ousted by Rory O'Connor, who was now the high king, sought support from Henry II, which ultimately led to Ireland becoming divided into Anglo-Norman and Irish areas. It took over fifty years to establish a near-English administration. Towards the end of the twelfth century and into the thirteenth it appeared that the Irish and English would be able to get along. The period shows ancient Irish society had not given up its cultural identity but remained quite distinct. This difference has never changed; the clan has always been more important.

The behaviour of the ruling classes has always been transitory – they have been unable to devise a social system that is fair to all and lasting. It seems that some individuals have to assert themselves and in the case of Ireland in the Dark Ages killing, theft, slavery, and rape persisted, the objects being to brag, frighten, amass power, and steal land.

As previously explained the surnames Keary, Kearey, and its variant, Ceary, are anglicisations of the ancient Irish family name Ó Ciardha, a one-time minor kingship, acknowledged clan, known in central and southwestern, Ireland, with a Gaelic name still in use today. This is not to pass over, devalue or dismiss other derivations of the name, for there are many of equal or higher standing. Past generations of the greater family have not only changed the spelling of their name but their country, all to escape servitude, bondage and suppression, caused by stronger clans, bad generalship, the influx of settlers and just plain theft. Whilst writing I have stumbled over the: O'Conor, O'Kelly, O'Kerry (Irish Ciarrai or Ciarraighe) O'Kenny, and O'Cleirigh families, and others, connected with the people of Ciar.

The aim of my studies has been to find out my family's history, and it's not getting any easier. The object is to discover what part of Ireland I can most likely call home, and how past members of the family lived, played, and died. Along the way, perhaps, I may discover what part the family played in Irish history, which was and is very strong, whilst seeking out heraldic practices.

To help me I have personally sought Grant of Arms (08.03.2021) as the method to make my quest official and complete. Thankfully the application was granted, including emblazon and registration; naturally payment is necessary when lodging all such far-reaching applications. This has been done by including a great deal of research, finally engaging Timeline Research at the Institute of Dublin.

Acceptance by Ireland's Livery rested upon whether Thomas Kearey (1791-1860) was Irish and first sons through the ages (Thomas Kearey 1820-1867 born London; Thomas Kearey, born London 1842-1900; Thomas Kearey, born London 1881-1882) were part of the greater family, and this could be firmly linked by certificate and census. Fortunately they were.

The Office of the Chief Herald, held by Ms. Colette O'Flaherty, is housed in the National Library of Ireland's Department of Manuscripts and Special Collections. This office ensures that pronouncements are given proper standing and recognition. The total sum payable is divided. The first part allows proof of Irish connection to be made and for design work to begin to represent the family in the whole process, overseen by the Herald, Mr. Donal Burke. The second part is paid before Letters Patent are written and the final arms painted by the Herald Painter. This final payment was made in July 2022.

Researching my DNA was an important first step: deoxyribonucleic an acid is a polymer composed of two polynucleotide chains, the coil forming a double helix. The polymer carries genetic instructions for the development, functioning, growth, and reproduction of organisms, including many viruses, carrying one of the four major types of macromolecules essential for life.

The object was to find the race of people who first settled in Ireland. They would be communicating, using their language of Celtic/Gaelic. The presence of Early Mesolithic sites at Lough Boora in Co. Offaly and also along the Blackwater in Co. Cork indicates that Ireland could have been colonized not just from the north-east but also from the south (*The Origins of the Irish* by J. P. Mallory, p 49). The language during the Neolithic Indo-European of c. 3000 BC probably originated among the earliest farming communities in southwestern Europe (p 299).

My maternal DNA H5a and paternal Haplogroup H-P96 showed my ancestors to be one of the earliest Stone Age People – later, early farmers in the Neolithic period in Western Eurasia, in this case Ireland – to make the first sortie into Ireland, introducing a good start to my quest. It would seem to be clear that there were at least three migration streams, the latest being

Ukrainian, together constituting 80% of the Irish population with R1b male DNA.

By the turn of the 10th century AD the Gaelic speaking Irish, Scots, Manx, West Country and other lesser island's formed a common northern Celtic speaking group – a Y-chromosomal haplogroup R – M269 haplogroup, which shares a common ancestor with a single nucleotide polymorphic mutation.

In the future the hunt for connection, seeking the construction of a family tree, will be based on the developing science of genetic. Individuals may seek those connections to build their family's history.

The Mesolithic People came later, followed by the Bronze Age, introducing the Celts in 500 BC. Later one such group inhabited Kildare, believed descended from Chathair Mór, son of Feidlimid Fiorurghlas, High King of Ireland, who reigned for three years before being killed by Conn Cetchathach.

The introduction of Christianity to Ireland eventually brought about fewer minor wars and limited slavery, theft, homelessness and rape, while cementing family and clan bonding. To ensure a definitive recorded date I have given Christianity introduced into Ireland, in the Fourth year of the reign of Laoghaire, King of all Ireland.

Tomas Cardinal Fiaich, in 'The Beginnings of Christianity', chapter 4, page 41, states: 'Irish Christians were sufficiently numerous by 432 to justify the appointment of a bishop by Rome.' Ciarán mac Ainmirech of Clonmacnoise, one of Ireland's monastic founders in the sixth century, belonged to the Cenél Connaill, from which Abbot Colum Cille originated.

It is recorded that the origins of the family name 'Ciardha' are believed to lie in the wishes of the Irish Saint Ciar in about 620 AD, when Fiachra son of Ciaran died. Its Gaelic origin is black or sable, perhaps derived from black hair or dark complexion rather than the Scottish Picts' name signifying a people who painted themselves. The family became part of the Cenél nÉogain, ruled by Muirchertach mac Muirelaig, son of Éochaid mac Domnaill, king of Cenél nEogain, a large group of families descended from Eoghan, brother of St. Columba, elder son of Niall Noigiallach of the Nine Hostages (nine clans owing allegiance to the fifth-century monarch who founded the Northern Ui Néill dynasty).

The Irish had five Gaelic kingdoms in the fifth to eleventh centuries: Ulster, Leinster, Munster, Connaught and Meath, each with a High King. In that time Cairpre Gabra were not a powerful tuath but were 'descendants of Coirpre' the eldest son of Niall, occupying land in the middle of Ireland which bordered with Meath, ruled by the Southern Ui Neill centred on Granard, today's Longford, an area at that time bearing the first Christian centres in Ireland.

By the twelfth century they were beaten by Conmhaicne tribes and absorbed into the larger Annaly kingdom, where they were given shelter by O'Farrell's fortress, the O'Ciardha (Keary), descendants of Niall becoming established as lords of Carbury about the same time as the Anglo-Norman invasion of Ireland. (Margaret Dobbs, 'The Territory and People of Tethba' 1941 7th Series, Vol 11, No.3.)

The following shows clearly that King Ciardha of Carbury was a tribal chief of a group of clans or families which included Cerry, Celly, Cenny, Ceary, Ciarie, Ciarrai, Cary, and others, all related to Coirpre, eldest son of Niall, based around Carbury before and during the first century, well before the castle was built. Giving a list of surnames may be confusing in that family second names were not used until the late 11/12th century; individuals were referred to by common everyday expressions, impressions and objects. Later, biblical Greek/Roman names began to be used.

During this period in history, Aethelred II 'The Unready', King of the English 978-1013, reigned. Edmond Ironside was King of the English in 1016. Henry I was King of France 1031-1060. In 1031 the Ommiad Caliphate of Spain was dissolved. In 1034 Malcolm of the Scots died. Canute King of England lived from 1016-1035. King Harold Harefoot died in 1040. The period includes, according to The Annals of Tigernach by King O'Ciardha.

The Annals of Tigernach. (also, Annals of Ireland, 807 B.C. to A. D. 1178), by the Abbot of Clonmacnoise.This work, transcribed 1870-1885, titled 'Revue Celtique' by Professeur H. D'Arbois de Jubainville, Collège de France, was printed in Paris 1895, edited by Whitley Stokes 1830-1909. It consisted of a number of written works. I give two instances, to give proof and method.

1. Page 290: *Mael Ruanaid Ua Ciardha, ri Cairpri, do marbad do Gallaib Atha cliath isin bliadain sin .i. do mac Turnin 7 do mac Aedha Hui Ferghail 7 Cellach Ua Findallan ri Delbna*

moire leo beous tria mebail . (See T 1165-10) (In this year MaelRuanaid Ua Ciadha, king of Cairbre, was treacherously killed by the Foreigners of Dublin, namely by the sons of Turnin and Aed Hua Fergail, and also Cellach Hua Findallan, king of Delbna Mor.

2. Page 295. (Flann mac Donncadh's Ua MaelSechlainn do marbad O Chairpri O Ciardha (<<Fland, son of Donnchad Hua MaelSechlainn, was killed by Cairbre Hua Ciarda >>

Page 414. The men of Teffa, and the Munter Geradain, and the Cairbri Hui Ciada went on a raid into Offaly, and reached the glebe of Cell eich (leg. Cell Achaid?), where a defeat was inflicted upon them, and Hua Ciarda and the son of Mac Findbairr, chief of the Muinter Geradain, and a great multitude, were slain.

(See T 1176-16) Flann son of Donnchadh O'Maelseachnaill was killed by Cairbre O'Ciardha.

The following has been taken from 'The Annals of Tigernach,' written in 993 AD, translated by Gearoid Mac Niocaill, Electronic edition compiled by Emer Purcell, Donnechadh O'Corrain. Publication CELT Corpuss of Electronic Texts, University of Cork, Ireland. There were three parts covering mostly 489-1178 AD surviving from the 14th century (MS Rawlinson B488). The point here is that they mention O'Ciardha (Keary), king of Cairpre. Carbery lies at the very south-western point of Ireland, not so far from the city of Cork – the second largest city in Ireland. Districts of MacCarthy of More, of Muskerry, and of Reagh surround the city, hemming in Carbery to its coastline.

T 993-2. Mael Ruanaigj-ua Ciardha, ri Cairpri do marbadh la Firu Teftha.

T 993–2. Maelruanaidha O'Ciardha, King of Cairbre, was killed by the men of Teffa.

T 1000.5 Aodh O'Ciardha was blinded by his brother, namely Valgarg, grandson Ciarda.

T 1020-9. Cu Luachra O'Conchobhair, King of Ciarraighe Luachra, died.

T 10024-10. Maelruanidh O'Ciardha, King of Carbery, died.

T 1029 -2 A great loss of life on Lnis Lainne in Cairbre Mor where forty persons of nobles of Cairbre were burned alive including Aodh O'Ruaire, King of Cairbre and the superior of Drunclifff.

T 1046-5. Fearghal O'Ciardha, King of Cairbre, was killed by the men of Teffa.

T 1067-5. O'Conchobhair of Kerry, King of Carraighe.

Luachra killed in Connacht.

T 1138.2. Mathghamhain O'Conchobhair, king of Ciarrsighe and of Corca Dhuibhna, tanist of the king of Munster, rested.

T 1138-5. Dealbhna Mor, wherein was slain Domhnall O'Ciardha, king of Carbury.

T 1145-9. The defeat of Dun Dubain by Murchadh O'Maclseachlainn and by Cairbre O'Ciardha on the men of Breifna, where 300 men fell, including Searrach O'Connachtaigh and Cathal O'Cathluain and O'Cumrain.

T 1150-1. The Giolla Claor O'Ciardha, King of Cairpre, felled by the Ui Faelain.

T 1155-5. The Giolla Got O'Ciardha, King of Cairpre, was killed by Donnchadh O'Maelseachlainn.

T 1165-10. A great war between the Meathmen and the men of Brefne, and Sitriue was killed by the Ui Ciardha and by Cairbre.

T1174-10 Mael Ruanaidh O'Ciardha, King of Cairpre, was killed by the Foreigners of Dublin in that year, i.e. by the son of Turnir and by the son of Aodh O'Fearghail and also Ceallach O'Fiondallar, king of Delbna Mor.

T 1176-4 Two score of the English were killed by the son of Giolla Padraig O'Ciardha.

T 1176-13. Domnall Mac Giolla Padraig, king of Cairbre O'Ciardha was treacherously killed by O'Maclseachlainn.

T 1176-16 Flann son of Donnchadh O'Maelseachnaill was killed by Cairbre O'Ciardha.

Unfortunately The Annals of Tigernach in 993 AD have not been quoted in Wikipedia to mention that the Giolla Got O'Ciardha, King of Cairpre, was killed by Donnchadh O'Maelseachlainn. Later, Donnchadh's son was killed by Cairbre O'Ciardha, maintaining history between 993–1176.

The old Irish root 'ciar' or céir 'dark', means perhaps black or sable. Tigernach mac Cairpri (d549) was an early Irish patron saint of Clones (Co Monaghan) in the Province of Ulster.

In 1090, the Annals (gospels) reported the Book of Kells returned from Donegal, in the kingdom of Midhe, the ancient territories of Mide, 'the midland part', and Brega ruled by King Finnechta Fledach. The king (or 'toisech', Irish for tribal chief) ruled over a people (Irish túath) responsible for the well-being of the tuath. The law tract Crith Gablach (early eighth century) says 'ri' (cognate with Latin rex a regendo dicitur) because he rules (rigidly). Ireland had over a hundred kingdoms which means that a tuath was relatively small. It was divided into nobility, freemen, scholars, lesser freemen, and serfs. Neither towns nor villages existed before the ninth century; people lived together in a caisel, an enclosure of stone. (taken from *Medieval Ireland*, by Michael Richter).

It must be remembered that the settlement's social structure, those inside, were extremely primitive, crude and uncouth looking for spiritual salvation in a whole variety of made-up acts and beliefs. The only qualities the people looked up to were brutality, crudity and coarseness, which offered some sort of security to weaker souls.

In descent from Cairbre Mor, meaning first or senior, son of Niall of the Nine Hostages a branch of Cenel Cairpre included Ua Chiardha (O'Keary, O'Carey) of Ui Cairpri Laigen in Carbury, County Kildare. With a location of county, Barony or Townland 'Crioch Cairpre Droma Cliad of northern County Sligo and north-east County Leitrim in the Barony of Carbury in north Sligo. Cineal (kingship) uibh Neill a' Tuaisceart. There is some indication that the Ui Neill kingdom in the area of County Kildare did not exist before the 12th century, of Ua Cairpre being driven from north-east Longford and Offaly (i.e. Cairpre Gabra) due to pressure from Ua Ruaire of Breifne and the Conmairecne expansion in the region.

The annals cite for Cairpre Laigin (Ua Chiardha between 954-2 – 1176-16), that 'Ualgarg Ua Ciardha King of Cairpre killed Cetnach son of Flann king of Luige.'

There is no doubt that the O'Ciardha were a paramount family in early Ireland; a kingship which slowly became reduced supporting the losing side, to be finally crushed by King Henry and later Cromwellian forces. Reading between the lines 'The Annals' give a sordid record of ancient Irish clan life – basically, killing each other, stealing one another's cattle, taking revenge, all to advance ownership, popularity and power.

As John Grenham records: 'The history of Ireland is a great drama of war, invasion, plantation, immigration, emigration, conflict, and solidarity.' This rather sums up Ireland and the Kearey family.

Carbury Castle. The ancient land of Mide (Offaly) was ruled by dynasties including the O'Ciardha ri Cairpri, King of Carbury - in the first millennium inhabiting pagan burial-places which remain there today. - Barry Raftery 1944-2010. Elizabeth O'Brien, *Mapping Death.*

My application for Grant of Arms to the Chief Herald of Ireland has tested my Irishness, both ancient and modern, and my patience. During the research, I have gained greater knowledge of Ireland's ancient history, sought out who my ancestors might have been but not found out where Thomas Kearey came from before taking ship to England.

Heraldry is not restricted to the Western world. Its introduction began with the need to recognise who was friend or foe, when tempers frayed in the heat of battle. Shields and helmet crests were carried and worn in the thirteenth century, when the practice of embroidering armorial ensigns on the surcoat worn over a coat of mail introduced the term 'coat of arms.' Letters Patent granted the Ensigns and Arms to the family. The Norman pointed shield (escutcheon) contains the figure, or design painted in colour (tincture) that form the 'coat of arms', in this instance the shield, divided (parting the shield's field), horizontally (per fess) as radiant, seen as flames in yellow, covering the bottom half of the shield (Or). This suggests flames from a furnace melting ore or heating metal – a family skill. The flames' background, black, (truth) defines in Gaelic, the use with 'Ciar,' connecting it with the family's Gaelic name. In heraldic terms, black, written as sable. These two colours, sable and or' are the family livery colours.

Above the flames are four crosses remembering the four brothers killed in WWI and their Christian upbringing; their top half position on the shield suggests the family were living north of the River Thames. On top of the shield is a helmet with closed visor, appropriate for esquires – gentlemen-at-arms. On either side of the helmet are mantlings there is scrollwork or flowering drapery, originally there to protect the helmet. Arranged, on top of the helmet, is a slightly curved wreath, a chaplet of the two coloured livery silks wound round each other. Above the wreath is the crest, a demi-panther incensed rampant guardant, flames emanating from beside its mouth and ears facing the viewer. A panther also represents a beautiful woman and mother who is tender and loving to her children and will defend them, even with her own life. The animal is displayed with roundels of red (meaning fortitude), blue (loyalty) and green (hope), holding in each front paw a blacksmith's hammer once again making a link to past family skills. These are all armorial bearing, crest, helmet, shield, and overall design, suggested by the Herald taking regard to the life of the person from whom I claim Irish descent and the following generations. The scroll is the Herald Painter's design, and the motto was suggested by myself. Over time, the Ciarraige Tribe of the Eoganacht People moved south and west towards Co. Cork and Kerry, having travelled through the ages from Co. Sligo and Leitrim. This movement of people shows how transient life was when pressure applied by powerful neighbours caused fear and terror.

The Ciarrage tribes or 'black people' populated much of north-western County Roscommon and are believed to have been the lords of Airtech – the present day barony of Frenchpark. Their seat is Basilic, near Castlereagh. Early peoples of Desmond included the Ciarraige Luacha. Domnall was the son of Muirchertach mac Neill and grandson of Niall Glundub. He was a member of the Cenel nEogain northern Ui Neill.

CHAPTER 1

The Kearey family

My fascination for finding out about my name, my origins and my place in Irish society has carried me a long way; to a number of books, websites, and the use of a good deal of paper, ink, and time – all which have given a good deal of information, alongside heaps of speculation and bucketfuls of doubtful facts. This is not good when you are trying to write a factual book about yourself and how you came to be. Therefore, I will have to bear up, and do the best I can, with the help of some equally dedicated authors such as J. P. Mallory, who gives a period of between the ninth and eighth millennia, before Ireland could become colonised, as temperatures rose and the ice fields of the last glaciation melted.

The creation of our world's surface involved the formation of ridges, crusts, plates, grinding and grating together to form the crust, with movements, fusions and mergers – all cooling sufficiently for water vapour, expelled by volcanic activity, to fall as rain and make the world habitable. Later these landmasses formed into continents, with ice-sheets and warmer periods, as postglacial corridors opened up, just before 4000 BC, known by historians as the Neolithic period. Wandering nomads, hunter-gatherers moving up from southern Europe, travelled through Brittany, using land bridges to make their way into a new world beyond.

One has to start somewhere, so I have chosen the land in the south-west corner of Ireland. Here these wanderers waded northwards from one patch of dry land through a swampy clump, skirting some rocks, to find a way forward to the land which became today's counties: Kerry, Cork, Limerick, Galway, Tipperary, and Waterford, all having access, to either the Atlantic, the English Channel, or both, by numerous bays and inlets.

It is important to remember that if you have Irish family connections and are not monied, poverty, starvation, homelessness and emigration will have played a major part in your family's psyche that never recedes. I pick up my pen again, to write another page of Kearey history, imagining the scene before me.

My maternal H5a and paternal Haplogroup H-P96 are given as belonging to one of the first hunter-gatherer groups of settlers from Gaul who gradually moved into the heart of Ireland. This weathered and tanned wandering tribe with related families were northern Celts of the Caucasian race – which included ancient and modern Europeans. Those who made their way to Ireland were part of the northern group of the race. This family, and other family groups, moved to where food and water could be found; they organized communities, which gave the group permanence. They had finally grown tired of roaming, especially when they could see there was sufficient food available to them where they were, and decided to stay to build permanent dwellings – pole houses made with animal skins, thatch and turf. They formed family groups; clothed in animal skins, they used stone, antler horn, wood, flint and shells as implements and stored grain, seed and nuts.

As soon as any human being around the world sets up home, they call that place their own and are prepared to fight over it. Toolmakers of the Neolithic period were the people who began the Bronze Age, which in turn became the Iron Age as other smelting ores were discovered and developed. Hammering iron hardens the metal, reheating allows shaping, and this manipulation allowed special farming tools, weapons, and implements to be designed and redesigned as challenges demanded. The latter part of Iron Age, which dated from c750 to AD 43, was the period when the Romans occupied Britain.

All groups of people seek leaders, to give them confidence, reliability and safety. Leadership is usually won by the most powerful; generally outspoken, confident, opinionated, and strong-minded people who give hope to the many for a better future, leading to the occupation of better farming land, more cattle and a greater access to food. However, this improvement creates jealous, unhappy neighbours who see the difference and want success for themselves. Future battles, thefts and homelessness create bad memories, causing interfamily wars.

There was, and always will be, a body of people who wish to assert themselves, show-off and be leaders, those who seek status and position and who pander to those in charge to improve their position. The leader – king, lord or chief – demonstrates his competence by improving the status of the group, achieving more growth, whether it be in land, produce, buildings, cattle or slaves. This basic human instinct travelled up out of Africa and southern Europe, becoming part of normal life in Ireland too. To give security the leader had to be obeyed, be adaptable and wise, holding those he led ready to pass on to the next generation. But throughout history, leadership has faltered, failed and become corrupted. Even a system of elections is no guarantee of continuance. A limited time in office must be set before re-election becomes necessary, to show competence and reliability and demonstrate greater social advancement.

The river Suir, which runs into an attractive valley, forms, with the Knockmealdown Mountains, the southern border with Waterford. Celtic people from Gaul pushed into the land, taking over Neolithic, Bronze and Iron Age cultures during the second half of the first millennium BC. They built up and established many small kingdoms called 'tuatha'. This race of people – from the kingdom of Galatia, originating from the Upper Danube, Italy, and Spain – formed the northern branch, and ruled from their future capital, Dublin. Their land extended over all Ireland and Wales, western and south-western Britain up England's western coast and its islands and onwards into Scotland.

The majority of these people were farmers and stockholders

working small rectangular fields and operating a cross-ploughing technique. They built dry-stone boundary walls and drainage ditches, lived in timber roundhouses or pole-houses and stored surplus grain in pits. Ireland's people lived in a land of mountain and forest, bog and grassland, and were never far away from well-stocked lake and grazed pasture. The people calculated their wealth by the size of their herds and the amount of land under cultivation. As with all human communities, other living things, natural climatic events, and the universe as they saw it, all gave imagined and actual causes for fear, leading to belief and reliance in gods that needed subservience and 'payment'. The human species needs hope, and relies upon gods and spirits to provide it.

The Celtic race

The Celtic race relied upon the bards – the High King's soothsayers, who foretold the tribe's destiny through poem or story. They were the purveyors of myth and legend, who passed on aspects of community which drew the people together. They were members of the aristocracy and did not sit with the musicians, entertainers and mercenaries near the door but alongside a raised dais, close to the lords' table. These bardic singers and storytellers related tales of heroes and gallant deeds; they were honoured and feted. It was a form of entertainment which included the broadcast of news, everyday events and tales of the past. As an important side issue, they introduced hope and confidence. Bards educated listeners in the facility and use of language that brought people together, instilling common cause and continuity; it gave the people a sense of belonging that lasted for generations. The religion – a cult built upon nature and ruled by druids, priests and prophets, later called 'Brehons', maintained influence by occultism, and a knowledge of seasonal changes - of things affected by the calendar, sun, wind, and rain. Any matters the Brehons could not explain they put down to something poorly performed or untimely.

The Romans never invaded Ireland, although they did stop the encroachment of Celtic people in Britain. Gradually the Roman influence inflicted a pressure that forced them back – a socio-political and economic force rather than a physical one. The Romans, assessing rightly that the Celts offered no real threat, continued their march northwards, leaving their expansion into metal-bearing western areas until later. The army that made up the Roman force was Germanic, an altogether stronger, fitter, and more advanced people than the Celtic farmers and stockbreeders. They were a tried and tested body of people from a number of tribes, hardened by their transient life – fighting, building roads and bridges, organizing logistics. The Celts were no match for military forces and tactics.

Ptolemy listed, in the second century AD, the names of Irish people in the P Celtic form, which was the language of Britain and Gaul. This group of people recorded by him were the Cruithni, linked to the Ciarraige ('Ciar') tribe of Connacht and north Kerry, in the land of the Mumu later called Munster, and in particular the northern half of counties Limerick, Tipperary and Offaly. These three counties were bordered to the north by the

River Shannon, which feeds two loughs, Derg and Ree. Inland, south of the river, the gentle rising land sweeps up to a range of mountains: Mullaghareirk, Galtee, the Slieveardagh Hills and Slieve Bloom, then down into the central plain of Carbury.

The early Christian church had as one of the Twelve Apostles of Ireland Saint Ciaran Saighir (the Elder). He was the first bishop of Ossary – one of the four who preceded Saint Patrick. He foundered Seir-Kieran, County Offaly. Ciaran, with a C or K, is an Irish personal name meaning 'Little Dark One' and thought to be related to Ciar, who was son of Fergus, King of Ulster. The name 'Ciar' is synonymous with Ciardha as being one of Ciar's People of the Ciarraige tribe. I will refer to this Irish word repeatedly during my search for connections. The advent of Christianity not only promoted peace, settlement of quarrels and hope but also transferred power. It was this power that became weakened; it could not give guidance or assertiveness when firmness was demanded. Abbeys, monasteries, nunneries and priories are in the main closed communities.

The Atlantic sweeps into the mouth of the Shannon until it reaches Limerick, under two bridges past the salmon weir onwards to the entrance of Lough Derg at Killaloe. South of the estuary of the river Shannon, its river and loughs, lived a tribe recorded as the Medon Mairtine. Over time, it was weakened by war and by encroaching raiders and neighbours – the thrusting Eoghanachta, a southern tribe expanding northwards. These people flourished, and like all tribal groupings it was made up of extended families, some closely related others not so, but all contributing to the main group.

The ruling suzerain or High King held this land bearing a cashel, a term used to describe a stepped walled settlement, referred to as a stronghold. All leaders relied on a hierarchical system based on obligations owed – obligations to pay for protection, farm the land, take part in social gatherings, contribute to clan activities and share benefits. These obligations, once accepted, were never withdrawn in life or death, and continued through the succeeding generations. The leader, Muiredach (325-355), maintained his position by strength of arms proved in battle. His position was no sinecure. Extended families were large, particularly the chief's, and there were always those envying his position and perhaps disputing his leadership, so he always had to be on guard.

Muiredach's son Eochaid (356-365), married Mongfind of Munster. From this union, future kings of Connacht reigned. His second wife Cairrenn was daughter of a Saxon king and an ancestor of the Uí Néill, prince of the Connachta. She was also mother to Niall NoínGiallach of the Nine Hostages 379-405, so called because nine tributary tribes owed him homage, who was High King of Erin, Ard ri, (The Gaelic form of High King, referred to as King of Tara. Niall eventually became one of the supreme rulers of all Ireland and founded this dynasty.

The marriage of Eochaid and Cairene brought together an alliance between the Saxons, Irish, and Picts, a royal line called Uí Néill (descendants of Niall). This continued for almost a thousand years until broken by Brian Boru, King of Cashel, who, although reigning as King, like others afterwards, never ousted the name and fact of Uí Néill, who represented true national identity. When Niall died, Connacht and the kingship of Ireland passed to his nephew. His sons, Eoghan, Connell and Enda, took over smaller parts of the kingdom in northern and central-southern Ireland. It was Eoghan of Aileach who now ruled as High King of Munster and from his eldest son was born Fiacha. It was in this fashion that the Eoghanacht line was born.

Ailill the King is vanished
Vanished Croghan's fort:
Kings to Clonmacnoise now
Come to play their court.

Aileach ruled from a great stone castle built on a 600-foot hill, and this was at one time the stronghold of Bronze Age kings. A treaty was drawn-up between all the clans, to divide Ireland into two parts, the dividing line passed between Dublin and Galway, part way following the river Shannon. The King of the southern part was the High King of Cashel, which was situated in a fertile plain. His seat, as King of Munster, was perched on a rock holding a stone fort built in the 400s. St Patrick (432-459) preached there, converting Aengus, the then King. In 1101, it passed into the hands of the church, which bestowed it to Murtough O'Brien.

Osraighe or Ossory covered the present county of Kilkenny and the southern portion of Leix, populated by the Ciarraige tribe. 'Ciar' refers to a nondescript colour which could be black, grey, brown, or tan and could describe the people's clothes, hair, or skin. It is also a family name, becoming part of Ciar's

People. They became vassal people owing allegiance to the Eoghanachta, who were the successors of the holy Cathach tribal lands, including all affiliated clans with similar names and family connections. The clan was under the royal protection of Ui Neill, descended from the Connachta, after Ciar Culdub was killed.

The hierarchy of kings was adapted to the older structure of provinces – Ulster, Munster, Connacht, and Leinster. Within these there were two kings vying for supremacy. They were competing for the revenues and title – provincial kings claiming lordship over lesser kings, among whom were the forebears of the O'Ciardha. Often these kings had to fight to enforce their claim, although each admitted the supremacy of the High King of Ireland.

From a heraldic point of view, 'Grant of Arms' makes reference to the generally accepted origin of the name Kearey or Ceary to the Irish word 'Ciar', combining this with heraldic devices that tell a story of the Kearey family starting with Thomas (1791-1860), who was born in Ireland. It is important to relate that whenever family trees are involved proof by certification – birth, death, marriage, and census – is essential, and In that way the Kearey, family arms and motto, 'Truth be told', can be included in the wider context of the name. However, that does not dismiss, disregard or belittle the existence of many other Ciardha/Keary/Ceary families throughout Irish history, nor does it dismiss previous generations going further back still to the first millennium.

It is almost impossible either to work out the dominance of

one particular tribe over another or to form a linearity of leading clans, especially if you try to put a date to each. It has to be pure conjecture, for there are no compatible pieces of evidence to back them up. All one can do is assess the likelihood that this was so, 'at the time of'. Britain's fifth century history revolves around the return of the Roman Army to Italy and the disintegration of almost five hundred years of Roman influence. The roads remained, the buildings suffered from lack of maintenance, but the language and social mores remained, to be adapted. Irishmen were to some degree unaffected by the turbulence which followed the Romans' retreat back to their homeland.

Christianity spread from the monasteries of Gaul, reaching Ireland at about the same time. It was then that there were great changes to the Irish Celtic language; church scribes began to record the life and times of the people, recording opinions and facts.

By about 540, the monks had begun to take over some of the power of the Brehons. Bishop Finian of the Ulaid of Dal Fiatach died of the plague 12th December 549 according to the Annals of Ulster, after the foundation of Cluain-Eraird in 520, 'Clonard in Meath'. By then, St. Ciaran of Seir-Kieran, St. Ciaran of Clonmacnoise and Columba of Tir-da-glasi were in their twenties. St Ciaran of Clonmacnoise, from Connaught, was the founder of an abbey near Lough Ree, and Columba, the greatest of the later generation monks, who founded over twenty religious houses, looked to him as their chief and ruler. St Ciaran was another of the Twelve Apostles of Erin. He died on the 9th September 546 at the age of 32 and was buried in his little church attached to the Abbey. Queen Devorgilla helped found the monastery on land gifted by Diarmid Mac Cerbhaill. Previously Queen Devorgilla had been given as tribute to the Fomorians (a term used to describe seaborne raiders, probably Viking) but rescued by CuChulainn, who offered her to Lugaid of Munster, High King of Ireland in about 500, but Lugaid refused to accept her.

Clonmacnoise was an important centre for learning and religious teaching, having its individual stone cells, its chapel and graveyard enclosed behind a circular stonewalled stronghold in Cashel. These descriptions are handed down to us from stanza, scriptures, hymns and the "Annals of Ulster." The rural society at this time was not one based upon towns or villages but ring-forts, lake dwellings, and later, monastery-settlements. The people within lived in much cruder constructions with little or no stonework but simple pole houses, often with an open roof, built on an earthen mound with ring ditches and offset entrances.

Ireland's history is about many small kingships that were always battling with each other and stealing each other's cattle. The advent of religious conversion did suppress these petty differences, for the preachers understood that they only upset the inhabitants, caused dissent and disturbed the flow of conversions during the period 530–540 – the time of Tuatha, ending in the second order. Finnian, 'the best of saints' - was the greatest Columba, both king and bishop. This great age of Ireland lasted three hundred years.

Most rulers had a very strong link with the church, and a clan chief could also be a priest, as could a lord – one position did not have greater importance than the other. It would not be cynical to suggest that clan chiefs saw this as an easy way to achieve salvation, and the church saw it as a means of converting the chief's subjects. These positions of power could all be headed up by the same person, or by a member of the same family, so it became very convenient. It is not surprising that some families held these offices for generations.

Irish Christianity had a great influence on Britain and records cannot be interpreted without some recourse into pagan Ireland and its traditions. Irish history, through the language of the bards, is much older and far more developed than England's, its neighbour to the east, although later history needs reference to early accounts by the Romans particularly Ptolemy, and later Christian writings by priests and leaders like St. Cianan. We have to be grateful for the visiting monks who stayed and had the necessary foresight to record what they saw and heard. It is only by this that we can form and date some events.

A generation later a daughter was born to king Duibhrea, and by her later good works, became canonised in about 645, about the time of Cogitosus, the biographer of Brigit. Ireland became the centre for monastic life. Finnian and Ciaran had coeducational foundations. Widows – and due to wars there were many – unprotected single women and girls were lodged as equals in monastic schools. The unstable society created many displaced unattached females who needed shelter and sustenance. Irish monasteries promoted arable farming and the instruction of good farming practices, for many relied upon their ordered existence, to provide food and safe lodging.

CHAPTER 2

Saint Ciar, 620-679

Ciar, St. Virgin, daughter of Duibhrea, died 679. Annals of the Kingdom of Ireland 'The Four Masters' translated by John O'Donovan, compiled by Emma Ryan. Adomnan of Iona, Life of St. Columba. The common Irish place names headed by Kil-(from Latin cella 'cell') point to a monastic origin.

Saint Ciarda School, c1949

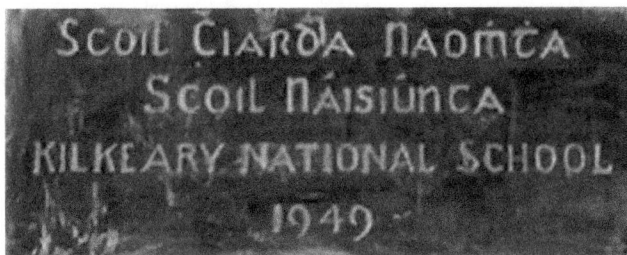

Kilkeary School Plaque

Kilkeary Church Cemetery

The inserted picture shows what Kilkeary Church looked like originally.

The Archaeological Inventory of North Tipperary, 8.9.1995, gives 1864 Kilkeary. OS21:14:6 (416, 13) 'Kilkeary Church (in Ruins)' OD 300-400 19172, 17572, gives church and graveyard. Situated on a south-facing slope in pasture. Described in the Civil Survey 1654-6 (Simington 1934, vol. 2, 263) as being ruined 'the walls onely standinge'. A ruinous church (dimensions, 9m N-S; 29.3. E-W), roughly centrally placed within a graveyard, aligned E-W and outlined by wall-footings (max. Height 1.1m) and collapsed limestone rubble. The present length is misleading; a low stonewalled burial plot appears to have been added to the west end. The original length was closer to 20m based on a description in the Ordnance Survey letters (O'Flanagan 1930, vol, 1, 199). An obelisk has been inserted in the east end of the church. Visible tombstones in the graveyard of William Carroll referred to in the OS letters date to 1706. There are no prepared cut stones; original work repaired in places.

Kilkeary Church is listed in the Record of Monuments and Places of North Tipperary with the number TN021-074001- https://www.bit.ly/2ZX0Wdb/. Historical and Technical information by Archaeologist Caimin O'Brien, National Monuments Service, Nenagh. Received 0-7-8/01/2020. The above link will take you to the NMS online description of the church with bibliographic references and photographs, all available for download.

The poor condition of Cill Ciardha (Church of Keary) makes it impossible to be certain about the date of the present surviving building, but it is most likely to date from the 12th/13th century. The mention of cyclopean masonry is interesting and could suggest a date around 1000-1100 AD, but the presence of large stones rarely indicates an early date for the church. The present building was built as the first parochial church of the parish of Kilkeary, on the site of the 7th century nunnery founded by Saint Ciar. The poor condition and meagre remains of the church building make it difficult to be certain about dating this structure. One can only put the condition of the ruined church down to theft and rotting roof beams. The church and graveyard are now in the care of Tipperary County Council, and there is a local graveyard committee called the Kilkeary Burial Ground Committee which looks after the site on behalf of the local parishioners.

National Monuments Service (NMS) received 07/01/2020: The precise location of the nunnery has never been identified. The most likely scenario is that the present stone church has been built on the site of the nunnery, although there is no archaeological evidence to support this. It is possible that the nunnery was located at another site within the townland of Kilkeary. The 7th century nunnery was originally built of timber and surrounded by an earth and timber enclosure. The construction of stone churches did not commence in Ireland until a few centuries later. No archaeological excavation has been carried out near the church.

Kilkeary Parish c1600: Irelands National Monuments Service

In 1901, surnames in Ireland became altered to simplify the translation of the Irish form into English, for example. the 'y' ending in English replaced aigh, aidh and dha. Keary surnames are numerous in Co. Tipperary, Dublin and Westmeath. The addition of an e to the y (ey), as in Kearey, emphasis the ee sound, a way to assume greater Englishness adopted by immigrants hoping to find work and to achieve greater assimilation. Latin was incorporated into Gaelic in about the 6th century. By the twelfth century, the language evolved into modern Irish. In the next century English began to be incorporated increasing word power.

Saint Ciarán of Clonmacnoise, who belonged to the first generation of saintly monastic founders, died in 549 AD, over seventy years before Saint Ciar's birth. Columba, Abbot of Iona, died twenty-three years before and Abbot Adomnán twenty-five years after her birth. These recorded facts give us a time-span. St Ciar was born over three generations after the arrival of Christianity in Ireland. She was revered by her example, her teaching, her saintliness and personal traits afforded her with enough strength to go on and promote her religion and beliefs on a wider scale.

St Ciar was a native of this district, and her father Duibhrea was descended from the line of Connors, Kings of Ireland. To her father's name was sometimes added 'insula', an island – this refers to an island now called King's Island, surrounded by a branch of the Shannon called Abbey River. Lough Derg's southern side is in the Province of Ormond, where St Ciar was born. Her great sanctity and many miracles attracted numbers of holy women to share her monastic life.

The name of this district was written by 'The Scholar of Aegus' as Cill Cheire, the church of St. Kera or Cera (Church of Keary); it is situated in the ancient Muscraidhe Thire, the Upper and Lower Ormond. In Aegus is written 'Ciar Ingen Duibhrea' referring to St. Ciardha, daughter of king Duibhrea, who was the local clan chief.

The O'Ciardha was one of the family groups that made up the Muscraidhe Tribe which populated central and south-west Ireland east of the river Shannon. The aristocratic family Ui Raibre is thought to have owned Cell Cére (Kilkeary). St. Ciar, who was also of the family, founded the church and nunnery.

What is important about this story is that it introduces my Irish name and it is St Ciar that I have to thank. My name is an abbreviated form of Máel MacGioha Ciar – 'as one of her devotees or followers'. The family name Ciardha/Keary was established from the naming of the saint in about 650 AD, making a close connection between the church and the secular head, king Duibhrea or Duina, reflected in the early writings.

John Colgan, Ireland's national hagiographist (writer of saints' lives & legends). Bibliography: Colgan, Triadis Thaumaturgae (Dublin 1996). Sharpe, 'Medieval Irish Saints' Lives: An Introduction to Vitae Sanctorum Hiberniae (Oxford 1991). C. Plummer ed. Vitae Sanctorum Hiberniae (Dublin 1997), gives: "That at the request of St Brendan, patron of Clonfert, this holy virgin, St Ciar, by her prayers, extinguished a pestiferous fire which had broken out in the region of Muscraidhe Thire." Saint Ciar, an abbess, founded her nunnery in Tipperary, north Munster, the area now known as Kilkeary, north Tipperary. It would appear that St. Ciar, by her name, family associations, and will, provided the use of her name to create Ciardha.

St Ciar's nunnery grew to house thirteen postulants in about 645 AD. This settlement, in Upper Ormond, appears to have been the only one established during the early Christian era in that area – later defined as 'in the diocese of the bishop of Killaloe'. With this number of nuns, there would be a back-up number of helpers, friends, relatives, workers, crofters and supporters.

There must have been a considerable population in and around the nunnery – a monastic community so described by Dr Richard Sharpe in the Life of Columba.

According to Omnium Sanctorum Hiberniae, a book dedicated to the saints of Ireland, we commemorate Saint Ciar as patron of the parish which bears her name – Kilkeary. County Tipperary (today's crossroads, graveyard and school). John, Canon O'Hanlon (1821-1905), gives us an insight into this holy woman and monastic foundress. The Parish of Kilkeary is in the Barony of Iffa and Offer East in the Diocese of Lismore and County Tipperary. Dr Richard Sharpe gives a most readable account of the life of a saint in his book Adomnàn of Iona, Life of St Columba.

Life in a religious settlement is described in the Life of St Columba giving us an idea of the building and surrounding land, the nuns sitting round the fire, reading religious scripts, a guest house where visitors could stay and a storehouse needing to be restocked. The cemetery had graves marked with a stone and the erection of a cross. All these early buildings and their uses can be easily imagined as very little different from life in any community of the time or place. BBC Time Team programmes have ably drawn a picture of the period. St Ciar's nunnery, perhaps supported by king Duibhrea, would have been a centre of the community.

Monks arriving from other European countries had a knowledge and understanding of Christian teaching and Latin.

They were there to persuade the Irish leaders to adopt a superior way of life. To do this they glorified God, explaining that salvation earned would give the converted everlasting life. They were successful in their task, giving themselves time and place to settle down and to build a base. It was a natural progression for the monks to copy the bible and religious tracts to regularise the curriculum and to help their mission forward. It is from these early writings that our story takes shape.

The religious order began to take over some of the power of the Brehons. Finnian died in the plague about ten years after the foundation of Clonard. By then both Ciaran and Columba of Terryglass were in their twenties. Saint Ciaran of Clonmacnoise from Connaught was the founder of the Abbey near Lough Ree and Columba, the greatest of the later generation of monks, founded Iona. St Ciaran was another of The Twelve Apostles of Ireland. He died on the 9th September 546 AD, at the age of 32 and was buried in his little church attached to the Abbey.

The rural society of this time was not one based upon towns or villages but ring-forts, lake dwellings and later, monastery-settlements. The people populated smaller communities of much cruder construction with little or no stonework but simple pole houses often with an open roof, built on an earthen mound with ring ditches and offset entrances.

Life for the Ciardha family was based upon the group or sect following the accepted position of the chief or head. The senior or chief would have won his position by strength of arms alone. His position was not automatically passed down to his son but offered to the strongest in arms. Young men won their spurs in the group's hierarchy by the number of cattle stolen or greatest fear wrought upon a neighbour. Common security was awarded by promised payment guaranteed by bond, so it was case of 'you look after me, I will look after you, and we will share any prize/spoils together'. It was a rough, tough world with no quarter given.

Ireland changed dramatically when Mac Erca (Muirchert ach mac Muiredaig, died c. 534) was High King of Ireland). Up to the twelfth century, the monastic bodies were all under the Rule of Columba 544 AD. St Ciarán was one of a number of Benedictine monks who were the first saint-founders. Between Mac Erca's death and the arrival of Patrick, Christianity became the established power base, governed by bishops. It was during Mac Erca's time there were mass conversions covering all Irish society. Several of the bishops stood up to the power of the lords, and probably the greatest of these was St Ciarán, the 'smith's (carriage-wright's) son', from Enda's Aran who founded Clonmacnoise, Co. Offaly, in 545 AD. He was one of the principals of the synods of Meg Léne at the time of 'Diarmait the Good', one of the great kings of Ireland. Columba commented wryly at the time of Ciarán death:

Blessed is God who called Ciaran from this world in his youth. If he had lived to an old age, he would have aroused many men's hostility.

Most rulers had a very strong link with the church – a clan chief could also be a priest, as could a lord, and one position did not have greater importance than any other. It would not be cynical to suggest that clan chiefs saw this as an easy way to achieve salvation, maintain order and hold onto their positions; the church saw the close connection as a means of converting the chief's subjects. If a member of the same family could hold these positions, then it all became very convenient and worthwhile. It is not surprising to find that some families held these offices for generations.

What was important to the common people was that the coming of Christianity reduced the incidence of vandalism, theft, and petty war, giving stability and greater unity. Eventually this gave the church equal if not greater power, which has lasted until today. In England it was that power – controlling land, buildings, gold, obedience, sanctity, even the gift of everlasting life, that forced Henry VIII to allow him to do as he pleased.

St Ciar's church was elaborately decorated, especially around the altar; the walls were painted to depict the apostles and the single roof span was covered with split stone slates. For the period, this represented a building of influence and authority, a dwelling that catered for a number of nuns, visiting pilgrims and for the needy, particularly women. The land close to the church was adopted as a burial ground for the local clan, still there today for all to see.

Kilkeary today is a parish, in the barony of Iffer and Offer East in the Diocese of Lismore and County of Tipperary, a Province of Munster, four miles south-east of Nenagh, on the road to Cashel. It comprises 2524 statute acres, and the land is generally good and mostly under tillage. Greenanstown House is the seat of Count D'Alton. The parish is a rectory, forming part of the union of Ballynaclough and corps of the deanery of Killaloe. The ruined nunnery and today's graveyard and school sit close to the crossroads, a microcosm of its past life.

The family O'Ciardha (Keary) was formed about the time St Ciaran died in 549, when Columba was a young man. The following list gives the family connection.

The Northern Ui Neill: Cenel Conaill. An early monastic founder was St. Ciaran of Clonmacnoise.

King Duibhrea or Duina, a minor king, Holy Island, North Tipperary.

Saint Ciar, canonized daughter of king Duibhrea b620 AD.

Mael MacGioha Ciar, (a follower of St. Ciar).

O'Ciardha – sept adopted family name. (Ciar – black)

St. Ciar, Abbess (monastic place name) Kilkeary, d679 AD.

Family, sept Cenel nEogain, king Muirchertach mac Muirelaig descended from Eoghan eldest son of Niall included Ua Ciardha.

Lords of Carbury.

Maelruanaidha O'Ciardha, king of Cairbre d993 AD.

Cairbre O'Ciardha maintains family history 993 – 1176 AD.

Abbot Adomnan of Iona, belonged to the Ui Neill his successor Conamail died in 704.

The O'Ciardha of Cairbre were poets of Clan Niall.

The young men of the family in ancient times were putting themselves in danger by stealing cattle to the extent that there would be fights, injuries and deaths, which would leave young women without security. The society had a surplus of young women who gladly found succour at St Ciar's nunnery. These women nursed the sick, fed the poor from food bred and grown by themselves, and tended the elderly.

The O'Ciardha clan was one of the family groups who made up the Múscraighe Thire, who populated central and south/west Ireland south-east of the river Shannon. The aristocratic family Uí Raibne reputedly owned Kilkeary close to Nenagh. St Ciar, who was also of the family, foundered the church. Cousins held the churches of Dromineer, Toomevara, and Kilaughnane. These religious houses were all close to the rich pastures that line the east shore of the river.

Written evidence of the time is unavailable, and later the scribes who did write of the times had no common language. We rely upon those Latin writers for Irish history, although they were far removed from the local people and their habits. Please excuse this writer too if my translation is faulty. The gap of two millennia casts long shadows and there are few surviving clues to go on.

One last explanation before I start. In the year AD 664/5 a Great Plague swept through Ireland, wiping out many monastic populations. The centuries between the sixteenth and nineteenth were equally destructive to both the population and clergy, during which the supporters of Henry and Cromwell later took their toll.

Other aristocratic branches of the family held smaller foundations, whilst some of the family settled at the great monastery of Birr. The Uí Daigre, yet another branch, held the church of Latteragh and claimed that Odrán, its founder, was one of them. Uí Léinéne was a family of Uí Daigre, and as late as 1074, the annals record the death of Gilla Brénnainn Ua Léknine, Superior of Letracha Odráin. The Ciardha clan lived in and ruled a large tract of central Ireland, were leaders of the church and provided armed men to support the High King of the period. Terryglass, Co. Tipperary was also an important religious building on the east side of Lough Derg fed by the river Shannon. The monastery was founded by St Columba of Terryglass. The Shannon and its lakes were circled by a number of communities all using their dugout canoes (coite or cimba) to plunder their neighbour's stock.

GPS: 53. 36157,- 6.96905: Carbury Castle between c1600–1700.The site is pre-Christian and holds a number of burial sites or barrows. The territory of Cairbre Ui Ciaidha was associated with the Lords of Carbury. Niall of the Nine Hostages was an antecedent of the clan Ciardha. After the Anglo-Normans the land was granted to a Norman, Meiler Fitzhenry, and later the Lords Bermingham built the castle. The ancient Irish clans lived in dispersed settlement sites across their clan territories. The Cairbre O'Ciardha clan territory was located in the barony of Carbury in County Kildare, which is where their settlement sites would have been located.

O'Ciardha or O'Carey, chiefs of Cairbre O'Ciardha (Keary) in the barony of Carbery in Co. Kildare, Seán Mór O'Dubhagáin (Duggan) (died 1372) wrote: "O'Ciardha are Cairbre of poets of the tribe Niall of Nine-Hostages." Poets were seen not only as learned men but as soothsayers and saviours.

The Religious Census of 1766 for Co. Tipperary has a number of entries for Thomas Keary, Daniel Keary, John Keary and Edmond Keary. One of these could well be the father of Thomas Kearey 1791-1860, my great- great-grandfather.

Rome provided Ireland with territorial bishops, each generally given a diocese close to a royal residence. As more and more nunneries and monasteries became established their incumbents became bishops, abbesses, and to some, great abbots. Most kings sought bishops for their own kingdoms, which gave them added power and influence. Sometimes when their requests were given at other times they were not, perhaps, allocated a monk under a bishop. The bishop, who was a monk, remained under the abbot, who was highly esteemed.

The southern church favoured conformity with Rome and the nunneries and monasteries were governed by many different groups, some as independent establishments. Unity was urgently needed, and it took the form of a metropolitan episcopate. The first candidate was put in place in 650 AD, in the southern see of Kildare, in northern Leinster. Ultimately, both north and south were united under Armagh, whose bishopric became Ireland's senior. Founded by Saint Patrick, Armagh remained the most important of all his monasteries. The Irish word for Abbot is 'comarba', meaning heir, so he is the heir of the founder. In many instances, the heir was also of the same dynastic family – the same kindred – the link between the founder and the patron.

A nunnery had much the same architectural layout as a monastery. The heart of the complex was still the attached cloister which ran around an open space encompassing most of the important buildings, such as the church, the refectory for communal meals, kitchens, accommodation and study areas. There might also be accommodation for pilgrims who had travelled to see the holy relics the nuns had acquired and looked after (which could be anything from a slipper of the Virgin Mary to the skeletal finger of a saint). Many nunneries had a cemetery for staff and another for lay people (men and women) who paid for the privilege of interment there after a service in the chapel.

The church did not suppress Gaelic (Irish) but retained part of it within Latin. The monastic libraries kept these works and preserved them. This liberal attitude was reflected in the church's writings but not in the religious services. Clerics used Irish in their studies and teaching, consulting a written grammar of the Irish tongue. Whether they knew what the outcome would be is not clear, but it made secular and clerical writing universally greater than English.

The monasteries and nunneries housed the teachers of Latin. Their ringed stone walls, built on a rampart mound, gave security and isolation from the unsettled land around. These cashels were every bit as defensive as the lord's castle, a place where the whole community could shelter. This was no haphazard arrangement but a place declaring wealth and power.

Books the monks copied initially had been written in

continental Europe. Trade flourished with the countries nearest to Ireland. This was not just normal trade between Britain, France, Spain and Ireland but religious sustenance as well. All religious houses had a scribe who attended to the matters of the day. In other times he copied out books of learning, which were circulated to create a library elsewhere. A Psalter, known as the Cathach and attributed to St Colum Cille, was written at about the time St Ciar was performing her good works. The Irish missionaries travelled on the continent, baptising Germans and Austrians and building up the faithful as they went. They went on pilgrimages 'seeking salvation and solitude', evangelising pagan peoples preparing a way for later monks to build upon.

It was not always the case that an Abbot was a bishop who governed a diocese or administered a tribe's territory; there was no such organization, and these things were interchangeable. This company of Christian women who formed the foundation of St Ciar's community in Upper Ormond in 645 AD, named after her, attending 'Cill Cheire (Church of Keary).' It was here that she ruled with considerable skill, increasing the postulants and giving the foundation credence and sanctity.

St Ciar's veneration was no trifling matter. To be officially recognised and canonized meant she was accepted by Rome and worthy of obedience. This allowed her to expect her followers, in matters of the church and women, to obey. Being a daughter of the king added to her power and prestige. This link between king and church made it easier to assume and hold onto power. This close association between the ruling body, either local or national, and the priesthood is a feature of early religious foundations. It was in both bodies' interests to have this close connection to keep power centralized and necessary, but also greatly assisting religious foundation.

When the nunnery at Kilkeary was well established and capable of self-regulation St Ciar left, accompanied by five nuns, to start a new foundation in North Offaly, King's County, where she obtained a site for another nunnery from St. Fintan. It was in a place now known as Tehelly, in the parish of Durrow, formed in about the year 655 AD. This was close to Clonmacnoise and St Ciaran's Church. The original foundation continued to flourish and minister to the local people.

Following the tidal river north from the mouth of the River Shannon, you come to a lough called Derg – the settlement of Killaloe occupies the land at the mouth to the lough. The great river continues through the lough northwards, to Clonmacnoise, a wealthy, sixth-century fort-like monastery built of stone, before entering Lough Ree, then onwards up to Carrick on the Shannon. It did not matter where St Ciar travelled, her title to property and obedience went along with her. She and the Bishop, who was the son of the king of Munster, jointly ruled the church. An early law tract refers to the bishop of Cork and Emly as uasal-epscop, giving them a status equal to the king of Munster, who was overlord of the southern half of Ireland.

Later, St Ciar (canonized pre-congregation) returned to Kilkeary, where she is reputed to have died of natural causes. Little is known of the subsequent history of the nunnery or of her burial place. Her death is recorded in the Annals of the Four Masters January 5th 679, Rewritten by John O'Donovan, LLD.,

M.R.I.A. Barrister at Law, Second Edition 1856. The following stanza is from Leahhar Breac, the Book of the MacEgans – Irish Pedigrees (Learned Brehons and historians) by John O'Hart, 1892 (fifth Edition) It seems quite remarkable that someone like St Ciar, who has recorded history, can be so utterly lost in historic scriptures that even the name is mis-spelled.

The call of Semeoin, the sage,
To Christ of purist…
A new, transitory, gentle nun was
Ciar, the daughter of Duibhrea.

It was in the middle and latter part of the first millennium that proper written records began to be kept. See 'The Irish Annals: Their genesis, evolution and history,' by D.P. McCarthy, senior lecturer in the department of computer science and a fellow of Trinity College, Dublin. The Book of Kells (illuminated manuscripts) was to be kept on the altar of churches and monasteries in ancient times and was written and illuminated c.800 CE. Rewritten by Joshua J. Mark. 'The lives of the Saints' was written in 1577 and first published 1579, by Skarga, another source of early recorded history written by scribes in Latin - the result of intended missionary zeal by Christian bishops and their scribes.

Gildas developed Latin literature in a style and order fit for publication. His paragraphs, sentences and words were impressions build upon the spoken word, placed together by sound and syllable. The language was from Europe but based upon English. As Ireland was the first large country to become Christian outside the Roman Empire, scholars had to write the Irish language in Latin characters and were compelled to write with an alphabet. Ogam notches became outdated in the seventh century Latin preserved the first written records. This is when the K was used, especially by mapmakers. Thereafter Latin began to be changed. English, Welsh and Irish were adapted and added to and developed into modern Irish modern.

Ciardha is the Gaelic spelling of the family name or clan - used by scribes in about 650 AD. Later writers increasingly used Cary, Carey or Keary as a more identifiable written form. The written Irish language was mainly derived from Latin and assumed closer integration to the accepted form of spelling and pronunciation in the sixth century - probably when the K was first used in written texts. In its softer anglicised form it is Cary or Carey, to make the difference less hard.

What era or part of the country 'K' rather than 'C' was used, is unclear. Perhaps the use of K (as in kick, in the Gaelic Q form) happened when the Gaelic Cill (church) was replaced by the Latinized Kil for place-names on maps – hence Kilkeary and Kilkenny. Most place names are in that form. The method of spelling might indicate who commissioned the work, when, and for what purpose.

The history of finding the right language and spelling of a family name explains what happened in Ireland that caused such disturbance and distress. The clan chiefs, Anglo-Irish aristocracy, their upstarts, the invaders, clerics and politicians may deserve censure for the chaos that marks the islands history, but the people certainly do not. The derivations of a name throughout the centuries give proof to the matter. In this instance, from Ciar to O'Ciardha, Cheire to Carie, Carey, Keary and Kearey.

This unity under Gaelic kings, represented by Ui Neill, continued for nearly two hundred years, until the Normans were invited to save the then ruling body. From this moment, Gaelic Ireland began to lose its identity and power base. This call to an outside body was to have far-reaching effects – ultimately not reversible. This was the downfall of Ireland. It allowed the Normans to assume not just power by invitation but 'of a right'. Richard FitzGilbert de Clare, 'Strongbow', promised payment for saving the Irish throne for O'Neill. Strongbow claimed in full, giving estates to followers and those who had supported him. By 1300, the Normans controlled most of Ireland.

The O'Ciardha (Cary or Keary) clan were a senior branch of the Cenel Cairpri, descended from the Cairpre who populated the central southwestern areas of Ireland, an ancient Gaeilge warrior kingdom speaking Gaeltacht. The chiefs of clan O'Ciardha were closely related to the supreme ruler of southern Ireland they were minor kings, ruling that part of southern Ireland located just below Lough Derg in today's northern Tipperary.

O'Cary rules over Carbery of bards,
He is of the tribe of Niall of the nine Hostages,
There are none but themselves there,
Of the clans of Niall over Leinster.

The main clan lands were Slievefelim or the Silvermine

Mountains and hills in the kingdom of Munster, not far from Ossory. The O'Ciardha was a senior group controlling a vast area related to Ui Neill. Another branch lived further east, inhabiting Carbury, Co Kildare. This extended family grouping, Cairbre Ua gCiardha, were also a prosperous family with many cattle.

The ancient site of St Ciardha's monastic house lay in a valley between Nenagh and Toomyvara, and the two mountains Slievekimalta and Devilsbit. To the north lie the Central Lowlands, an area of farms, market towns, peat bogs, glens and lakes. Before intensive cultivation began, the land was heavily forested. With the growth of many settlements the nearest navigable river influenced their development; in this case it was the river Shannon and in particular Lough Derg, five miles north of Nenagh; its southern banks bordered Lower Ormond and Arra and Owney. The family territory roughly conforms to the centre of the country, an area of hill and lowland. It was bog free downland, rich in minerals and well drained and hedged. This central part of the land was split between cousins into east and west groups. Unfortunately both groups suffered from having several competing branches, which weakened the power base. The eastern cousins' centre was at Cashel, and the other, the northern group, the Lower Shannon; it was over this area that the king had over lordship of the Ostmen of Waterford and Limerick, including their two important cities. This large area conforms roughly to today's Co Tipperary.

The central/southern Uí Néills, (Ui means 'children of', a term of gentility, ie those of the ruling family). This is a much older form than Ó or more strictly 'Ua'. O' means grandchild, linking to a previous generation. It was to this branch of the O' Néill's that the O' Ciardha clan became indelibly linked. The Keary clan were a 'sept' (meaning a clan, esp. in Ireland. 'Of sept' describes minor Gaelic/Irish ruling families or clans, or divided clan (clan, n. Scottish Highlanders with common ancestor, esp. while under patriarchal control. In early times individuals were known by one name only. As the population grew, another name was added – this gave individuals a family name. To then advance this system an O' was added to make an even greater linkage to a group or clan. As clans were displaced by interclan wars, splits occurred in the clan. Still keeping their name and traditions, families began to form in differing parts of the country. The stronger and more warlike the chief, the greater the pressure on his neighbour. After the first millennium AD the language formed into the written word for the first time. This noted social happenings and to whom – history was in the making. Irish dialects began to be developed, especially around main clan structures in particular counties.

This allegiance between the O'Neill's and the O'Ciardha continued until the latter lost all their clan lands over a period of six hundred years, ending at the same time as the restoration of Charles II, after Cromwell's death. (Planta, n. English settler, on forfeited lands in 17th c., person settled in plantation).

Edward Maclysaght's, 'More Irish Families', 1982, p50, agrees that the majority of those called Carey (or Keary) belong to the O'Ciardha, a senior branch of the Cenel Cairpri. It can be seen that whether C or K is used, the name refers to the same people.

In all research into genealogical connections within the O'Ciardha, certain names are always cropping up; in particular, O'Meara, O'Kennedy and O'Carroll. Toomevara Parish contains the districts of Agnameadle, Ballymackey, Kilkeary, Templedowney and Ballygibbon. It has three ancient ecclesiastical ruins, one of which was an ancient foundation for women established by St. Ciardha. There are also several ruined castles, some habitable, others not, being just ruins. The name of this district was written by the 'Scholar of Aegus' as Cill Cheire, the church of St. Kera, Cera, or Ciar (Kilkeary – Church of Keary) situated in the ancient Muscraidhe Thire, the Upper and Lower Ormond. In Aegus written: 'Ciar Ingen Duibhrea' meaning St. Ciardha, daughter of king Duibhrea. The cemetery was used by the Ciarraighe - Luachra tribe in Upper Ormond, not far from Roscrea and King's county.

The ancient church of Kilkeary was built about 625AD, and is 57 feet long and just over 19 feet wide. It is now in ruins, having had all its features destroyed except for a few massive stones, one of them weighing several tons. It was built in a semi-cyclopean style of Lange limestone rocks in the seventh and eighth centuries. In the graveyard is a monument to Major General Sir William Parker Carrol of Ballygrenade, a descendant of the O'Carrolls of Ely. In 1702, another member of the family was buried here. General Carrol was from Lissenhall, on the far side of Nenagh Town, and had a very distinguished career in the Spanish Army fighting under the Duke of Wellington during the Napoleonic Wars. He was highly thought of in England, and married an illegitimate daughter of King George III. William was also a politician who petitioned for the separation of the Northern and Southern Grand Juries in the county, in the 1830s. The fact that the Carrols used the Kilkeary graveyard – the site of the nunnery – was in keeping with Gaelic tradition. The Carrols, Kennedys and Meara were all inhabitants, south of the River Shannon. When the O'Ciardha were being harassed, then evicted, some transferred allegiance to the security of these families, who welcomed them as brothers in arms.

The nearest large town to Kilkeary is Nenagh, seven miles west; an important centre for its Anglo-Norman association and Franciscan Friary, which Kennedy founded in 1240, and Cromwell destroyed in 1650. It was one of the new walled towns designed in 1171, and the citizens, fearing incursions from warring factions, lent a hand with the building. The town council passed a law whereby every person, including: shop owners, priests and women was allotted a day in the week when they had to help in building the town walls. Toomyvara, a pleasant small market town, lies four miles east, lying astride an important crossroads.

The Vikings came in 795 AD. Scandinavians called Norsemen, most likely from Holland, pillaged and plundered coastline and river settlements around Ireland and Britain, building fortresses at Dublin, Waterford, Wexford, Cork and Limerick, the main towns of Ireland. These guardians of main river inlets, sometimes titled kings, were tribal chiefs or earls, and in no way could they be described as rulers of large tracts of the countryside. They lived in stone houses with a surrounding wall punctured by fortified gates. Circling this stronghold were a number of ditches and mounds with offset entrances. Finding Ireland particularly accommodating, the Norsemen chose the best land and settled, marrying into the population and becoming known as Ostmen. They felt at home in this pagan land of tales, songs, myths and legend – it was much like their own former homeland.

Since medieval times 'baile' has meant home/town, 'fearann' land/territory and 'aka' town land. These pre-date the Norman invasion and describe in Gaelic the smallest territorial unit. Some townlands, such as Kilkeary ('Church of Keary'), reflect the name of a person or family. In this instance it is St Ciar. The first maps on a national scale to define the Irish townland began with Cromwell in the 1650s. The boundaries of a townland usually follow natural features, hills or rivers.

National Service Records shows the Ancient Parish on its map held by the Monument Service gives the full boundary outline and also lists adjoining townlands. The first Survey of Ireland 1658 links with Down Survey maps, townland landowners. A population census will reveal old townland spelling variations, and other variations of historical names such as Tithe Applotments 1821-51, and Valuation Field Books 1824-56.

CHAPTER 3

The Vikings

⁓⸎⁓

Through the ages, a settlement on the river mouth was important. Later it would be called Limerick, and would come to play a vital role in the development of the country as a place well known for its salmon fishing and for its access up the river into the heart of the country. In Lough Derg, longboats were often at anchor, close to the shore, some drawn up on the beach, others hauled up onto logs for repair. These were the property of Viking raiders, who were frequent visitors, their coming and going accepted by the inhabitants. A number of the Vikings struck up relationships with the locals, married and had children, but they remained working the land and fishing. This convenient fraternization ensured a safe harbour, a place where boats restocked whilst taking on water. Like many immigrants to a new land, they took an active part in its development, becoming more committed to its survival than the original inhabitants, as the incoming Normans later found to their cost.

In the 830s, the Viking raids became even more extensive. They defeated the Uí Néill in battle and began plundering widely. The clergy were at this point part of the nobility and church property was protected by law. Monks could not act as security, nor make bequests without their abbot's consent, for the abbot was the administrative head of the church.

The Norse raids lasted until the 870s, died out, and erupted again. Ten years later 'the great Norse tyrant Barith was killed, but not before destroying Cianan of Duleek's oratory. The kingdom of Uí Failge comprised the baronies of Offaly in County Kildare and part of the diocese of Kildare, their kings being related to the ruling Laigin dynasty. However, the southern Uí Néill maintained precedence in Munster until the reign of Feidlimid mac Crimthainn in AD886.

In the latter part of the first millennium, the Uí Néill was probably the most important family grouping, dominating both the northern and southern parts of Ireland. They were descended from Niall Noígiallach, who himself was from Conn. The Vikings at the battle of Dublin (919AD) killed Niall Glundub, ancestor and over-king of the Uí Néill. During the battle, five other kings and many other nobles were killed. Glondub was related to Niall, the last of the kings of Tara, the legendary seat of the high kingship, ejected by Brian Boru when he rose to power. In 920, the Norse settlement at the mouth of the Shannon was enlarged and became the city of Limerick. It was the start of a flourishing trading centre, the beginning of the salmon industry and the restocking of many Viking boats. In 937, the Limerick

Vikings clashed with those of Dublin on Lough Ree and were defeated. The Shannon was of major importance in military campaigns throughout Ireland's history. The association with the Norse never diminished – eventually they become integrated into the Irish community.

The city was criss-crossed by wooden streets, houses and workshops. Mathgamaim sacked the city in 964 after previously capturing Cashel from the Eoganachta. All those he found fit to fight were killed, the others enslaved. His brother Brian later killed him.

The monastic movement established great ecclesiastical centres and one of these was at Kildare, in the early ninth century, where Uí Néill was appointed provincial governor by the monasteries and King of Leinster. He lived there with his brother, the abbot, and his sister, the abbess. The heartland of Leinster was the Vale of the Liffey and the valleys of the Barrow and the Slaney. At Domnach Sechnaill generations of the same family reigned as abbots; this fact gives light on how leadership of the church passed on to succeeding generations.

The Irish chieftain's allegiances fluctuated, depending on what they thought to their advantage. In this, the Ciardha clan was no different. It is frequently mentioned in the Annals of the Four Masters from 952 onwards to the death of Ua Ciardha tighearna Coirpre (O'Keary, Lord of Carbury), and again in 993 when Mael Ruanaig O'Ciardha, the then king of Carbury, was killed by the Teftha. This killing went on; the tribes were continually seeking a way to gain territory. In 1128, we finally read of the slaying of H. Ciardha ri Cairpri, another King of Carbury.

The kingship of the Cenel Eoghain weakened and dropped out of succession. By 976, Brian Boraime (Boru) had asserted control over the whole of Munster. It was during this time that the daughter and grandson of Amlaib Cuaran (AD945-80) were baptised and given Irish Christian names – Mael Muore and Gilla Ciarain. Later, during the Battle of Clontarf (1014), Brian heralded the claim to the throne of all Ireland, including the land held by the Ostmen. Support, however, was not forthcoming from other Irish leaders. A number of clan leaders populated north Leinster and Munster, one being Maelsheachlainn O' Ciardha, who was bribed just before the battle to desert with his men and fight with the Norsemen to remove Brian's power in Limerick. This united gathering failed, and Brian won a great victory, although he did not live long enough to reap the rewards, being killed in his tent pitched on the field of battle.

Boru's reign shattered the old order; his death allowed Máel Sechnaill II to be High King of Ireland until his demise in 1022. The Ostmen were given leave to stay and develop their towns, which gradually became main centres of importance. All those clans linked to the O'Neill's, including the O'Ciardha, lost political power and new relationships were formed; some gained advancement others declined. The O'Ciardha clan started to split up. Part moved to the kingdom of Man, others to the Isles and a further group retreated to western Munster, today's Counties Cork and Kerry, whilst others fled to the hills or joined other clans. The main nucleus of older members continued to maintain their old ways close to the ancestral home.

Enjoying large areas of land, or what it produced, did not

burden the Irish lord or leader. It mattered not to him that another might quote amounts; he was more concerned about status, based on whom he knew, who served him and who needed his power and position. This was a major failing in the Irish leadership system; leaders accepted the rank others accorded them, showing greater deference and accepting that the other was the greater lord. When Boru died, all that deference died with him and there was turmoil, until they all settled down again, more than likely to show a different order. The king was not a judge; he was there to lead his people into war and to lead the various meetings. However, it was rare that the eldest male descendant or nominated leader was not accepted. He had to be strong enough to demand obedience, having proved his worth with deeds. The pagan Brehons, previously known as the Druids, were the lawyers and governed the social system. They were not the poets or filid, although holding the same high office.

Kincora was a stone-built fortress guarding Lough Derg and was at one time Brian Boru's capital, although Cashel still represented the ancient seat of the Munster kings. Boru first established himself as King of Munster in place of the traditional Eoganacht King of Cashel in 1002. Mael Sechnaill, King of Tara, who had been ruling since 980, acknowledged his supremacy. Two years before, High King Murchertach had presented Kincora to the Church, becoming the seat for the new archbishopric of Munster. Gilla Espaic, or Gilbert was made Bishop of Limerick in about 1106, and appointed papal legate. This action made an alliance between the High King and southern reformers to the traditional head of the Irish Church.

The O'Brians moved to their new capital in Limerick, ruling the Ostmen – their vassals. At Limerick, called by the Norse name, the 'Lax Weir', that salmon fishing was highly valued becoming a chief industry – many Viking ships rode at anchor in the Shannon lakes. Ostmen, meaning 'Eastmen', the name given to Christianized semi-Irish settlers in Ireland after 1014, were an established entity before the invasion of England by the Normans.

The waves of the sea and the salmon depicted on the bottom third of the family coat of arms suggest that the sea that feeds the River Shannon and Lough Derg played an important part in the life of the family - sufficient to be recorded on the O'Ciardha shield.

Murchertach divided Ireland up into twenty-four sees in 1111. This action replaced the old monastic order. Eight years later Turloch sought high kingship after Murchertach's death. The O'Brians and the kingdom of Cashel never assumed great power again. Turloch had his fleet based on Lough Derg and his fortress at Dunleogha, which held Connacht and the bridges over the Shannon. Turloch had twenty-three sons, and all had land at the expense of others who were taken on as vassals or thrown out. The aristocracy was so avaricious and so numerous that there was no other outlet for them but war. Munster was divided between three of Turloch's sons, Murchertach, Diarmait and Tad, who died within a month. Tribe extinction by war, expulsion, or ill health was commonplace. About thirty years later, with the advent of the Cistercian Order, peace was restored.

Turloch More O'Connor, 1119–1156, was the next High

King. He was the son of Rory O'Connor, King of Connacht in 1106. Ireland contained a hundred kinglets arranged into five bigger groupings roughly matching today's provinces. The High King ruled one of the provinces and held the power base of the others. In Ireland, there were three grades of kings. At the bottom was the king of the smallest kingdom, called a tuath, next in order was an over king, Ruairi, and finally the king over kings, or ri. By the middle of the twelfth century, these titles had changed to lordships. Lower down the social scale came noblemen linked to the lord - normally by a feudal bond, owing an allegiance. At the bottom of the scale came the commoners, some freemen, others not. Where a clan inhabited a border area between counties or shared land with the diocese, which was the case with the O'Ciardha-Killaloe, the likelihood of that clan remaining strong was slight. Wars and disputes undermined ancient rights, especially when the warrior chiefs were away fighting; weaknesses were soon exposed. This describes what was happening to clan lands, why clan chiefs had to be 'on their toes' to cover their rear whilst they, and their main fighting men, were away serving their senior king.

THE MACLOCHLAINN KINGS OF CINEL EOGHAIN
Murchertach (High King) 1156–66

Connor	Niall	Melachlin	Murchertach	Connor Beg	Donal
1166–70	1170–76	1176–85	1188–96	1201	1230-81

It is clear that the O'Ciardha clan chiefs were 'vassals' under the protection of another – in this case it was the O'Neills. They in turn had vassals, and so on. If one or another lost power there was a readjustment. If one clan was split up through inter-clan wars they lost status; in some cases the clan became extinct, their land and rights forfeited. For clans to survive their chiefs had to demonstrate their strength, usually in battle. It was necessary to have allegiances to ensure security. The O'Ciardha were part of the Eoghanacht, as were the O'Sullivans, O'Donoghue, O'Mahony and possibly the O'Carthys, as well as others. It is impossible to say which was the more senior or who was most favoured.

The Irish clan system worked through the rent of land – the chief owed his position to an overlord to whom he paid either cash, cattle, service for the land, or all three. He was expected to supply men to fight the lord's battles and to give support and succour – safe haven, in times of defeat – all to contribute towards 'payback'. Every family in the clan did similarly towards the clan chief. In its simplest form it worked well, but when it grew more complicated the system broke down, especially when there was nothing to pay or barter with to settle the sum owing.

This hieratical grouping of families with a corporate entity gave a political and legal involvement recognised by those around them. A single person or group could represent the clan as long as they had political influence or property. Over a period, the clan rulers multiplied by birth and marriage, by so doing displacing those lower down the social scale. Even though you were of the leader's family, this did not guarantee your position.

The clan system revolved around a 'common people' based

within an identifiable area of land, say, a valley, and it was accepted that a particular man's claim to noble rank and apparel was established over many centuries. When the dynastic clans covered the population of this area and its founder was accepted as their common ancestor, the chief was born. To marry outside the valley and the community was a rarity. The clan law in Ireland was a customary law, which was slightly different from Scotland and Wales.

The obviously more powerful Normans, whom Sechnaill showed devotion to, particularly towards Henry I, dominated the ruling bodies in Ireland. It was in 1163 that Giolla Ciaran O'Draighnan died at the Abbey of Fore, a year before Abbot Moel Coenighin O'Gorman. Six years later, after the subjugation of the native Irish by the Normans in 1169, Strongbow married Aoife.

Domnall Mac Lochlainn, King of the Uí Néill, had total power over southern Ireland until he fell from office (the Ui Neills of Meath and Ailech ruled for over 500 years). Domnall lost his power after appealing to Henry II for help. The English invasion was sanctioned and authorized by Pope Adrian in 1155, led by Henry's Cambro-Norman barons under the call to invade and help Domnall reclaim his land. Henry allowed Dermot to recruit sympathisers among the Norman barons of Wales. Between 1169 and 1171 the Cambro-Normans, under the Earl of Pembroke, Strongbow not only seized all of Leinster and Dublin but also invaded neighbouring provinces, defeating Rory O'Connor, High King of Ireland. Land was seized in the guise of payback for help received. Henry II demanded and received fealty and tribute from all the surrounding kings. There followed a further diminution of the clans, and O'Ciardha again elected not to show fealty, although he was a liegeman of Ui Neill.

From about 1170 onwards, the English began to colonise Ireland. This was to the ultimate detriment of the old order of Gaelic kings; they were never to rule their own provinces again. It was from this point that clan O'Ciardha began to diminish once more. Their lands and titles were stolen and distributed to English sympathisers. In 1171 O'Connor and O'Carroll, with others, were defeated in battle by Strongbow, establishing the Normans as supreme. In 1175 Kerry, Limerick, Clare and Tipperary, the kingdom of Limerick (land of the O'Brians), was signed away by Henry II and given to Philip de Braose. Munster then became more French than any other place outside France.

In 1183-5 Gerald of Wales in his commentary 'Topographic Hiberniae' described Ireland as being a land of bogs, wood and lakes. This was about the only factual thing he wrote about Ireland and it was true for most of the north and central plain, at least for the next five hundred years, until land clearing and cultivation took place. What Gerald did predict correctly was that 'Ireland would not be conquered'. He noticed that the natives' fighting skills improved with time – they put up a greater organised resistance as new fighting skills were learned and old strongholds strengthened. This was certainly attributed to the old order. In 1189, Conor O'Connor, son of Rory and the last native king of Ireland, was turned out of Connacht and slain. His son Cathal Carrach, known as the Red Hand of Ireland, claimed the kingship, as did Rory's brother Cathal Crovderg. De Courcy eventually recognised him as king of Connacht. When Ruaidri Ua Conchobair died in 1198, to be buried in Clonmacnoise, Gaelic Irish power ended. Limerick was fortified by the building of King John's castle on the shores of the Shannon, to quell O'Brian's kingdom of Thomond. Thirteen years later in 1202 Crovderg, brother of Ard ri, 'of the Red Hand' (the O'Ciardha clan motto is the same), was inaugurated king by ancient ceremony at Carn Fraoich. The English considered him the greatest of all the Irish kings.

Kylkeary is considered an unwalled urban settlement. It had many streets and numerous inhabitants – Irish as well as immigrant English. It traded in wool and hides and supported itself through the sale of vegetable products. The church and nunnery provided a visiting place for travellers passing through. It covered an area of many hundreds of acres and Nenagh, its closest manor town, now owned by Butler, had 'incorporation' conferred upon it – a privileged position. The charter granted that any tenement held for a year and a day was owned, and if by an Irishman, to be declared 'free as an Englishman'. There was of course an acceptance that one did not openly declare and display too many old Gaelic customs.

Towns like Nenagh began to be built up with gated retaining walls. Forests were felled and new methods of agriculture developed. Masons and stonecutters were enticed to construct the walls and houses, helped by the inhabitants, who mixed the mortar and carried the stone. The citizens' help was not always voluntary, even though it was for their safety. Laws were passed forcing the population to assist in the work. No one was left out of the labour force; all had to give a hand. If a man could not work because of illness or work having to be done in his own business, his wife had to take his place. Nenagh felt secure and the town prospered. Churches were extended and rebuilt; education was ordained as being necessary. English laws followed, and a degree of prosperity was felt.

The English language became the common means of expression. Art and science were adopted, together with the administration of finance and justice. Anglo-Irish dynasties gradually assumed the ruling hand; enclaves created frontiers which undermined the old feudal nobility. Many of these Anglo-Irish families still occupy seized lands to this day. A continuing feature in this subjugated and colonised land was that the colonists never thought of themselves as being natives but Englishmen. The Irish annuals describe how King John tried to ensure good relations with the natives but fell out with the northern king Aed us Neill and the Connacht king, Cathal Crobderg Ua Conchobair. Both paid homage, but neither trusted King John.

CHAPTER 4

Clan land

Between 1219 and 1232, Richard de Burgh's nephew Hubert was temporarily in charge of England. This gave Richard considerable influence in Limerick and Tipperary, which gave him a good base from which to conquer and subdue Connacht, which he proceeded to do. All this occurred close to the clan land of the O'Ciardha, who had cast his lot in with O'Connor. The Munster chronicle reports for 1248 that 'many of the kings' sons of Ireland' were slain that year. There was a great deal of killing and raiding, endless campaigns, fire-raising, cattle raids and pillage; the land was in turmoil.

The Lordship of Leinster, partitioned between the five daughters of William Marshal, husband of Strongbow's daughter Isabel, resulted in Kilkenny being given its liberty from the crown. This was at the end of the thirteenth century. Another change just prior to this was the rise of William, Baron of Naas and a tenant of the lords of Leinster. The lordship of Ireland was granted to Edward I in 1254 and continued by his son, who died in 1327. John Fitz Thomas of Offaly, Earl of Kildare, passed on the earldom to his son Thomas. In 1258, the sons of the king of Thomond and associated nobility including the O'Ciardha met and conferred supreme authority to Brian O'Neill, who was unfortunately killed at the abortive Battle of Downpatrick in 1260.

One of Strongbow's knights, Hugh de Lacy, one of the largest landholders in Hertfordshire, was granted the province of Meath, part of Longford and Offaly, for the service of fifty knights. He in turn distributed lordships – entire baronies and sub-divisions of manors – to his followers, who proceeded to erect fortified enclosures to protect new immigrants. Not all this went down well with the inhabitants. In Limerick and Tipperary, a sheriff was installed to collect revenues, impart judicial opinions and command military powers. This pressure further pushed the O'Ciardha clan into the hills and inaccessible places. The sub-division of land and the installation of overseers created an outpost for the barons to protect Leinster and Dublin from incursion and provide a jumping-off place to subdue outer regions of southern and western Ireland.

In 1297, Tipperary County was required to send an elected representative to attend the Dublin parliament – towns within the county two years later and of both by 1300. This act had the effect of displacing the old order, the Gaelic Irish - the Gaelic nobility. The Normans took over, marrying into the Irish leadership and developing the towns and cities for their own.

Enormous progress was made in the task of integrating all the population into the new community. Forests were cleared to form cultivated land and new methods of agriculture introduced to produce more food. Trades and commercial enterprises were contained within the newly built walled towns, like Nenagh. It was a period of prosperity, which allowed monastic houses to flourish. This progress was later reversed.

Fore Abbey, Collinstown, Westmeath, the largest Gothic Benedictine Monastery in Ireland with 300 monks, dates back to AD 630. Inside is an Anchorites' hermitage cell of c1500. The river Boyne rises off this hill to the south, which offers a good view over the great central plain. Within sight are the ruins of at least four castles, all built by the De Berminghams.

A few years later a Gaelic reconquest swept away many of the Anglo-Irish ruling bodies, their manorial systems and associated village settlements. The old forms of address, writing, and reference were returned to and life reverted to the way it had been before English rule. This pattern, the old order, tried to reassert itself but became crushed. These times introduced the first of the galloglasses (the term means 'foreign warriors') who were the 'bondsmen' – the mercenaries of the future. They came originally from north-west Scotland and were afterwards used by the Irish, acknowledging their usefulness. Their recruitment, of any number, could be from a single clan or a number of clans – especially clan leaders without land, home or roots. The lord had to be able to keep them and their families, providing food and a dwelling. This was a very expensive undertaking, so few were taken on. Using huge axes like the Normans and protected by chain mail, they acted very much like samurai, who, experienced in war, gave protection and allegiance unto death. They joined forces with O'Connor, who sought help from King Haakon of Norway to oust the Normans from Ireland and become King. The plea came to nothing, for King Haakon died before a landing could be made. Another attempt was made by inviting Edward Bruce of Scotland in 1316, but this too failed after causing mayhem for three years, and Bruce was killed at the battle of Faughart. The great plague – the Black Death, which had already laid waste to the population of Europe – struck the country in the winter of 1348. Friar Clyn describes the result as the depopulation of Kilkenny, to the extent that 'there is hardly a house where there is only one dead'. The people thought the end of the world had arrived. Certainly nothing was the same afterwards. If there was any disputed land or a family death which made inheritance impossible, the land went back into the holdings of the lord of the manor.

In 1354, Lord Ormond granted land to O'Meara near Toomevara. Four years later another parcel of land was granted to O'Kennedy, only this time the land was in the manor of Nenagh. It appears these two clans had been granted all of Lower Ormond and part of Upper Ormond, the O'Carrolls, Murrough of Uriel, the chiefs of Ely and other prominent families connected to the O'Ciardha clan. These two clan families, the O'Carrolls and O'Kennedys, occupied land which bordered and overlapped ancient O'Ciardha territory. In law, when a clan was without land, its legal claim to clanship was revoked.

The 'Statutes of Kilkenny' passed by the Irish Parliament in 1366 prohibited colonists from intermarrying with the native Irish or learning their language. This change unsettled the population and created in its wake absentee property owners who did not want to return to 'a land of unrest'. By 1364, there were considerable financial problems caused by these absconders. Thirty years later King Richard II created the first of a succession of Irish kings of arms. He wanted to control all those areas that the native Irish had reasserted their office in – their way of life. Heralds needed to marshal the arms of the various knights, give military advice, and regularise the battles. This was the start of a continual feud. The Gaelic Irish, Anglo-Irish and Normans began to unite to form a united front against England. And the 'Irish question' began to assert itself…

In the towns and villages of Ormond, which included Kilkeary, the Anglo-Normans had to negotiate and deal with local cultivators or freemen and the serfs called betaghs. This was similar to the English manorial system only not so efficient. In Ireland, the people were bought and sold with the land. Everything, their labour, animals and produce, was taxed.

Eventually, the Anglo-Normans tried to oust them and take over their property, for they did not understand them nor want to integrate with them. They had tried to emancipate them, but they would not pay the fee. However, they still wanted their labour, which they needed. This created a lot of bad feeling and resentment. Niall Mor O'Neill, King of Tir Eoghain, was optimistic that he would be promoted as the English crown's representative over all Ireland, to bring about stability. It was not to be. After a considerable number of unsuccessful expeditions, battles, and disputes, Niall Garbh O'Donnell died in 1439.

By 1430, the original Irish lords occupied only the less fertile parts of the country. Those that did were no match for the Anglo-Irish, who operated intensive farming methods. They were doomed if they continued to try to maintain the old ways of living. They were not slow in adopting a more conciliatory tone, gradually assuming alliances both by marriage and sharing common goals. They began to drop the right to govern like lords. The White Earl of Ormond, who was related to both Mac Murchada of Leinster and Ua Neill of Ulster, held Tipperary and the majority of Kilkenny. Ireland was a land divided between the Anglo-English lords, as the Butler earls of Ormond, and the highly divided Gaelic world of ancient custom, language and local chiefs. The effect this had on the English crown was great, for it occupied the attention of Richard II to the extent that Henry of Lancaster landed in England and seized the throne. Richard's sally into Ireland in 1399 failed to unite the land under one king. There was no other landing in Ireland by an English king during the Middle-Ages – the 'Wars of the Roses' had taken all the energy and finances, making England weak. In the mid-1400s, the County of Meath, central Ireland, was split into two, English and Irish.

'The Pale' was a fortified earthen rampart built in the fifteenth century to enclose the royal administration lands of Louth and half of Meath and Kildare including Dublin. It became known as the Pale from 'palatinate' – the territory of a feudal or sovereign lord. Thomas Fitz Maurice (1456-78) was one of three surviving Anglo-Irish magnates. Previously, the Earl of Kildare had been the most powerful. However, the earls continued to assert their right to maintain their own land even when faced by intervention by Edward IV and Henry VII. The Gaelic Irish chiefs began to assert themselves, for they were now experienced in better ways of making war – they had benefited from previous struggles. This was not the time to build but to claim back lost land.

During these troubled times the chiefs were all in ferment. This was the Ireland of old – there were uprisings in the air and 'all was a-tremble'. Repairing the keep, replacing the fences and repointing the walls were for stay-at-homes; fighting was far more interesting. This inattention – ruination by neglect – was to happen to castles, churches and monasteries. Local people able to carry the heavy loads away and stripped the buildings of their lead, stone and wood. This demolition and destruction mainly affected the estates and vacant properties of absentee owners.

The Irish lords and military leaders still relied upon the long two-handed sword as their chief weapon of war for close fighting. To discourage enemy horses, ten-foot spears were anchored in the ground. The lancers resorted to short swords for infighting, whilst arrows kept their riders at bay. Chain mail, helmets and heavy coats protected their bodies, although they still wore sandals without stockings. How different this was to the mass of peasants who made up the army. Many were barefoot; none wore a headdress. They wielded axes, swords and clubs, plain and unfinished. Their strength came from knowledge of the country, which they could exist on, and they could bear the customary hardships.

It is important to understand that it was not always the case that an elder son or any son at all, inherited the chief's position. Naturally the chief, before he died, tried to ensure his son did take over his position, and to that end he trained his son in such a way that this would happen. That was not always the case. Quite often, when a clan chief died the elders asked for a vote – who they wanted to lead them – carried out by a show of hands. Normally it went to the strongest – the champion, one who could not be challenged. On the other hand, the old chief's lands were divided according to the seniority of the person – to the clan elders, not necessarily to his family and his sons. In 1534, Thomas, Lord Offaly, the son of the ninth earl of Kildare and leader of the Anglo-Irish, declared himself 'the king's enemy'. He was after the governorship of Ireland. That stirred up the pot of rebellion, which was again put down in no short measure by Skiffington, Henry VIII's representative.

Ireland had been a 'lordship' of the Norman English crown and in 1585 Hugh O'Neill (1540-1616) became second Earl of Tyrone, leading, with Spanish help, an uprising, which was defeated in 1601. After this setback Ui Neill, rather than submit to English influence, chose exile, as did O'Donnell and ninety of his followers. Amongst those to leave were O'Ciardha henchmen, who chose the Netherlands. Dermot O'Ciardha of Offaly stayed to create an opposition movement and to oversee the scattered clan families. The establishment in 1570 of presidencies in Munster and Connacht saw a push by the English to take a grip of the land north of the River Shannon. It had been a hard task to subdue the lords of Munster, who excommunicated Elizabeth. The lands of O'Carroll and O'Kennedy to the east of Lough Derg above Cashel, encompassing ancient O'Ciardha land, were not within the English marches until years later when The Connacht and Munster Councils of 1569-71 decreed it so. There was rebellion in 1579, which ended in the defeat of Tyrone, who surrendered four years later. Ireland was now a conquered land. Queen Elizabeth I had succeeded where others had failed.

The suppression of the monasteries during the reformation and the civil disturbances after wards led to the destruction of many church treasures. The churches of Keary and Fethard in Co. Tipperary and Askeaton in Co. Limerick were ravaged. Important statues and other treasures were destroyed, although some rare wooden statues, a bronze processional cross from Ballylongford, Co. Limerick and an embroidered cape from Waterford survived.

Another vast emigration to continental Europe followed. The English administration did everything in its power to anglicize the customs of the few remaining native Irish. The few Gaelic adherents that had survived the Tudor and Stuart Plantations were eventually ruined by the anti-Catholic legislation enacted by the Dublin Parliament after the victory of William III. These laws stopped estates being handed down to the eldest son; instead they had to divide them between all the children, which resulted, over time, to estates being whittled down to small freeholdings. The chiefs were unable to maintain patronage within their clans, which eroded the social systems - developed over many years. From that time, the clan system gradually wilted away even though the local peasantry continued to support the old ways. The process known as plantation began in the Tudor period, but mainly by James I, in Ulster and Munster, and led to the settlement of 40,000 Scottish and English immigrants by 1641. There was much more to come...both plantation and unrest!

In the Down Survey of 1646, the O'Kennedy, the O'Mera and the McGrath families, owned the land of Toomevara parish and Kilkeary. Many of the O'Ciardha clan were integrated into the O'Kennedys for protection, assuming their name and customs. The ancient ecclesiastical foundation for women established by St Ciardha was still a recognisable site, although by then a ruin. The suppression of the monasteries finished off what plantation had done before.

Migration from Britain into Ireland continued apace throughout the pre-Protestant years, mainly to areas, mainly eastern, which were fertile and had access to natural resources and the sea. This influx greatly improved social and material benefit from the skilled workers and farmers passing through, and had the additional effect of enlarging the knowledge and horizons of those who were involved. This caused a split in society, both religious and social. The clans were always at odds with each other, trying to gain more power and space. It was an age-old way of life which sapped the strength of family groupings and did nothing to advance society. Many families were being pushed out by the aggressive and vibrant newcomers – those given plantation lands. Many moved into Tipperary from neighbouring Leinster, gradually easing out the inhabitants.

Colonel Owen Roe O'Neill, a nephew of the great Hugh O'Neill, spent his entire career in the Spanish army of the Netherlands, and he was not the only one. At that time there was almost a greater alliance between the Irish nobility and the Spanish, particularly in the Netherlands, than between the English and Anglo-Irish. Certainly this existed with 'the old order'. Colonel O'Neill and Colonel Thomas Preston attempted to expel the Scottish Covenanters, who, unknown to him at the time, had connections with Cromwell's army. Needless to say, they failed.

The population of Ireland in the 1650s was now divided into those who were actively disloyal – the original native Irish; the old English subjects, who were now through intermarriage and assimilation, Gaelic and Catholic; and the newer loyal English who were Protestant landowners and titleholders and included the latest Scots settlers in Ulster. An Act of August 1652 declared that all the Irish and Anglo-Irish who could not prove "Constant Good Affections" to the Cromwellian cause should lose one-third of their estates, the remaining two-thirds to be made over as 'new areas for transportation'. The settlements changed the character of Ireland forever, and with that the landowning aristocracy as well.

'Ireland's Natural History', published in 1652 and jointly dedicated to Cromwell and Fleetwood, debated the possibility that Protestants from Europe were induced to settle the island. Cromwell's concern was that there might be either an uprising in Ireland or incursions from abroad – by Catholics. In this, history proved him right. There needed to be a new start in colonising Ireland by settlement, with reliable people – educated Protestants.

September 1653 saw a new Act of Plantation. This time grants were given to English towns to entice skilled tradesmen to immigrate. Adventurers were apportioned estates and the Army paid for in gifts of land. Whole areas were made over in this way to the English. Two-thirds of all Ireland was distributed, including all of Leinster, Kilkenny, Kildare, Kerry and Carlow; Kilkeary was not included, coming within the County of Tipperary (see County Map of Kylkeary). Other than a small strip made over to the English, Clare and Connaught were left to the Irish. Whereas this action was sensible as a way to control the population and prevent an uprising, it was undoubtedly immoral and caused great resentment. A quarter of Wicklow, Wexford, Kildare, Kilkenny, and Carlow was very English and had been for generations – since Henry, in fact. Everybody else was forcibly removed from towns and villages, compatriots and children included. People who stayed had to declare themselves Protestants. People with prefixes O, M, or Mac were banned, and their land forfeited. However, these Gaelic prefixes were allowed in Irish areas. In this manner great estates were built up by the English moneyed classes, who were in the main the ruling Protestant aristocrats and gentry. Many of these lesser English aristocrats continued to provide personnel for English armed services. Forty percent of all United Kingdom armed services, especially the army, had men with Irish connections fighting for them.

In Upper and Lower Ormond, and throughout much of Ireland, some of the old established Catholic landowning families, the O'Ciardha amongst them, took refuge in the hills and other outlying places to escape domination and subjugation to the Protestant forces. This broke up many of the clan families after they had lost their land. Eventually their legal rights were forgotten – and thereby forfeited – by lack of use, neglect, and absence. The descendants of the old order took their dead to ancestral graveyards in Ballinaclogh and Kilkeary, perpetuating age-old rights and customs.

CHAPTER 5

Thomas, head of the family

It would appear from documented sources that the name Thomas was always retained for the first-born son of the head of the family. Thomas O'Ciardha of Offaly, Fore, is believed to have belonged to a branch of the Cahill family of Connaught, derived from Cathal, number 102 of the Cahill of Connaught pedigree. He was also known as Thomas Baintreadhachd (Thomas the Widower) and was the ancestor of Keary of Fore, from Co. Meath.

In Hart's Irish Pedigrees of 1887, p499, Keary or Carey of Fore, Co Westmeath, was descended from Dermot O'Ciardha of Offaly. During the 1650s he reverted to the Keary form of spelling, because another member of the family, using the C, had become a Protestant. Today's Herald questions Hart's interpretation.

Thomas O'Ciardha was killed by Cromwell's Parliamentarian

troops in 1654, at the burning of Saint Fechin's Abbey. The monastery was an important monastic centre founded in AD630, later to become a small fortified town defended by two gates, a canal, a mound and a ditch. The monastery withstood several burnings and raids, eventually becoming an Anglo-Norman priory under the rule of the order of St Augustine. The last Prior, William Nugent, surrendered the house and possessions to Henry VIII. The town of Fore was allied to the English, being close to the English 'Pale'.

It was during the sacking of the Abbey that Thomas's three sons, Thomas the Elder, who married Mary O'Brian of Naas, niece of Hugh O'Byrne, Patrick, and James, escaped. They found refuge with Hugh O'Byrne of Dublin, one of the Confederate Catholics. In the early 1600s, the O'Byrne family owned vast estates round Clare, Naas in Kildare and Wicklow. Thomas died in Spain nine years later. Patrick entered Spanish service in the military, and Hugh married Margaret O'Brian, daughter of Dermot O'Brian of Naas. Their son John O'Brian married Mary, daughter of Owen M'Kewen of Clontarf and Swords. Their second child was a daughter born in 1749, who in 1780 married Hugh O'Moore of Longford, Castlepollard, in the County of Westmeath. The whole family were Catholics and held Gaelic allegiances to language and habit.

In 1653-65 Leinster was one of four equal land provinces of Ireland made up of areas such as Kilkenny, assigned by the English Parliament as security for soldiers and adventurers. Carlow and Kildare were kept as a government reservation, and Queens County was kept aside to be included in the plantations of the Catholic James I. The throne of England was, after James II, occupied by Mary and William of Orange – hence Irish Protestants becoming 'Orangemen'. This reign effectively destroyed the Catholic landowning classes.

The outcome of the Cromwellian plantation period was some Irish Catholic citizens selling up, others going demented with worry, some running away, and others being executed. The transportations were completed finally in July 1655. There were many arrests for failing to transplant, in fact so many that the gaols were full. Hangings made space available until an excuse was found to let some go. Those selected to be freed were the landowners, not the landless. A few years later some of the new owners sold up to others who increased their grants by purchase to become the new 'gentlemen landowners'. It was generally a clearance of the old landowners, and even in the Restoration things were never the same again – the old ways in Kilkeary were disregarded. Some old freeholders went to Irish counties whilst others went abroad, mainly to Spain and Holland, away from English influence, changing their names and making a fresh start. By this time, the clan was almost non-existent.

In the Civil Survey of 1654-1656, the Parish of Kilkeary was spelt Kylkeary, showing that even at that late stage spellings were still not regularised. This also suggests that the parish was considerably larger, containing several townships and parcels of land. The parish began at the ford of Bellasuillsane on the river Geagh, bounded with the parish of Kylnaneafe followed the river southward to Poellacholla, which adjoins Tampledony, Ballymacky, Grenanstowne and Lisbony. The parish was described in the survey as having good arable meadows and pastures, several springs and a number of plough-lands. The Hearth Money Rolls indicate that several members of the family living in Co. Tipperary started to use the English form of Ceary to retain their estates. They were better off under the Restoration settlement, for they received back three-fifths of their land. That was before the 1691 Jacobite War; by the end of it they had even less. Those of the family who retained their Gaelic native Irish names lived outside Clonmel's walls.

Many of the old gentry, including the O'Ciardha and the O'Kennedys, were evicted from their estates. In exchange they had been given 'fractions' – huts to live in, where they had to stay without possessions. One of the clans, the O'Kennedys of Ormond, had their 'fraction' confiscated in the Williamite wars because 48 of the clan families wished to maintain their Gaelic inheritance. This did not go down well with the Anglo-Irish, who expected them to conform. Other families, related to the old gentry, hid under another name for fear of losing what little they had managed to retain.

The O'Ciardha and O'Kennedys were not the only clans to live by deception. It is clear that few of the old families realigned back to their former allegiances. They had not been happy under the previous relationships and wanted to make a change. Some of the elderly stayed at home and worked for their new masters, tilling their own land; others wished to leave allotted land in Connaught. In Ormond, the more adventurous gentry took refuge in the inaccessible valleys of Glenculloo between the Slieve Felim hills, where their descendants still carried their dead to the churchyard at Kilkeary.

In 1659, Kilkeary, in the barony of Upper Ormond, held 769 households with a population of about four thousand persons. Kilkeary was a direct grantee land made over to a new sitting owner, James Dalton. Some years later, during the Restoration period, some of the transferred settlement land was retrieved by the old landowners, who included the O'Mearas, O'Connors and, Charles and Antony O'Carroll. Catholics held twenty percent of land in Kilkeary, Toomevara and Nenagh, but this percentage fell during the 1700s. In Petty's census of 1659, the O'Ciardha made up the largest percentage living in the Baronies of Scrine, Co Meath, and Ballybritt, south Offaly. The McCareys of Moycashel Barony, Westmeath were also in abundance. Ireland was a mainly Catholic population ruled and given its laws by an Anglo-Irish hierarchy. The country's link to Rome gave it its cultural base, which made it allied to the Continent through the Irish Colleges in France, the Italian military academies, and those businesses engaged in overseas trade. To the English the Irish appeared a threat, even though Ireland was a poorer cousin.

The Irish population in 1690 was now nearly two million and growing. Limerick was a prosperous seaport and used as a bastion against British influence; it was the last to hold out. The Jacobites used the town and its river to retreat. Limerick's city walls held, but only just. William confiscated all the land belonging to those Catholics who later escaped to France. The result of the defeat was the Treaty of Limerick in 1691, the third great defeat. In 1692 Thomas and Bridget Carey of Legbourne saw the defeat of the Catholic cause. A number of families were allowed to live there, retaining their property. They were considered docile enough, accepting English law; however, all Catholics were subject to penal laws.

At that time, there were a number of landholding and public office Acts that restricted the rights of Catholics, preventing them from assuming state office and property. If an individual wished to 'get on' – 'improve his lot' – he had to go where there was money to be made, skills to be passed on and property to be bought. That goal was accomplished by appearing to adopt the Protestant religion, translating their name into English, or adopting a more recognisable English name. This was the start of the giving up of the clan's Gaelic connection and the adoption of the more English 'C' or 'K' to spell Carey or Keary. By adopting these changes, they could hope to either live in a settlement area or find a new life abroad.

In the diocese of Killaloe, which included Kilkeary, there were only a few beneficed clergymen and even fewer actually resided in the area. There were about three Catholic priests to one clergyman. Churches were not maintained properly, allowing rotting roofs and broken walls to let in the damp and rain. This and the paucity of clergymen also affected other church property, including glebe houses and land. Idleness was also recorded when it came to tithe collecting and ministering to parishioners.

There was an exodus from the countryside, for there were few opportunities for the ambitious and capable. The landowners patronised the tenant farmers, who at one time had been self-supporting but now relied upon handouts and loans because of the potato blight. The problems were so acute that stealing crops was a daily event, to avoid starvation. Not long before, generations of families had lived together in harmony and occupied land not belonging to them, knowing they would not be evicted. Now the English Parliament was taking their land away. Economic fluctuations prompted by taxation upset the normal domestic industry, particularly the prices of seed, potatoes and livestock. These extra costs created unrest. Rebellion was in the air, and tensions increased in rural areas, releasing sectarian antipathies. There was a general collapse of Protestant morale. When looking towards the Catholic majority, the Protestants could see they were outnumbered. There were several threats, both real and imaginary, of invasion, rebellion and insurrection from France and Spain.

Tenant farmers, working from small farms in the diocese of Killaloe, mainly produced vegetables and corn, while larger farms grazed cattle. Previously leases could have been set for forty years. Farmers had made their own repairs and improvements, draining the land and rotating their crops. The landowners made sure their land was fully occupied so that it did not go to waste and become overgrown. Now when a farm became vacant, the new lease ran according to periods of prosperity or want – in times of plenty they were short term. The result was that tenants were not taking a long-term view of their future by planning ahead, keeping back some of their produce to use as next year's seed, planning the rotation of crops, or devising ways of improving the drainage by digging ditches and drains.

In the mid-18th century, the poor majority in Ireland lived in utmost poverty. Their accommodation was squalid, and their diets were made up of potato, turnips and a little wheat, milk and on rare occasions beef. The population was increasing at an enormous rate. It was only the narrow coastal plain that provided a market economy – here they managed to sell some of their produce. The poorer folk, living further inland up in the hills, depended on a subsistence economy. High rents were increasingly left unpaid, which generated debts, which led to evictions. The property owners forced the poor to pay an ever-increasing amount for rent; the interest rates on owed money continued to rise. The whole system discouraged improvements in property and proper farm management, particularly land drainage, fertilization, rotation of crops and animal husbandry using fallow land as a cushion for poor harvests. It was a self-generating national disaster which seemed to be unstoppable – and as it turned out, was.

About this time Daniel O'Cary adopted the Protestant religion and, wishing to anglicise his name still further in order to make a distinction between the families, asked for a meeting with the then head of the family to declare an oath whereby he would reassume the spelling of Keary - removing the prefix O and the use of C. Many of the Irish began to look beyond their local areas for employment. The more adventurous found that America and the Caribbean offered them more. America became an important land for Irish immigrant labour. The life appealed to many for its religious nonconformity and political independence. The American War of Independence started in

1775 and was an inspiration to many of the Irish poor to get back at the English.

CHAPTER 6

The family meeting

⁓⚓⁓

In the late 1770s, there was a widespread agricultural crisis. This was not the first time that this problem had occurred with the national food crop thanks to poor harvests, low cattle prices and the high cost of wheat, potatoes and milk. All this had been experienced before. The greatest problem for Ireland was that the population relied upon a staple annual crop of potatoes; where the English relied upon bread as their staple food, the Irish depended on potatoes. Corn was relatively simple to import and had a better shelf life. Potatoes needed careful handling from a suitable source and weight for weight was wasteful – it was also a difficult commodity to ship.

The enclosure movement caused further resentment. Rents increased yet again and there was a decline in wages; inflation was rife. A number of militant movements raised popular passion to influence the landowners and government to reduce rents, all to no avail. Taxation, tithes, rents and church dues were a continual grievance. Commercial cotton spinning and weaving were introduced into Ireland in 1777. Three years later modern machines and expertise brought over from England, established an enterprise which gave employment to many unemployed folk in towns and villages. This was the start of the great Irish linen industry.

O'Halloran, an Irish historian writing in 1778, gave O'Meara as a Lord Chief of an ancient house, descended from the O'Brien clan. Many of the O'Ciardha clan joined in his service with the Irish Brigade. A number of the clan then started to use the anglicised form of O'Carey, or O'Cary more often at the turn of the eighteenth century. Margaret Keary's second son Thomas Padrick married Julia, daughter of Roderick Murphy of Castledermot in Kildare, who had four sons, the eldest being named Thomas, as was the custom. He was the first of this family to stop using the prefix 'O' and to begin using the name of Keary. He married Mary, daughter of John Keogh of Castlepollard, an agricultural town in Westmeath, in 1815; John died in Dublin in 1836, and was interred in the churchyard of Artane.

The latest steam engines were imported from England to provide power for many of the mills, so no longer did the manufacturers have to rely upon water to drive their wheels. These engines required coal and allied services that in themselves created new business ventures, which prospered, initiating further capital expenditure. Heavy industries like mining, iron and steel producers, pottery manufactures, tanning, glassware and coach building all needed raw materials, delivered by road, canal, river and ports. These large building projects needed capital investment. Investors saw the opportunity to make a profit; they could see the outcome of an abundance of cheap labour and the profitability created by those first cotton mills.

This was a time when rural communities in villages and towns showed a remarkable turn inwards, towards collaborating and engaging in shared interests. These rural folk were in the main Catholics and spoke Gaelic, keenly aware that the city workers were 'a set apart' from their life in the village. Sporting events, fairs, markets, wakes, funerals, cockfights, hunting and field events abounded. These gatherings united people and stimulated political thought. Gradually the unrest grew until eventually nightly political meetings were arranged. In Tipperary, Neath and Limerick, under the pretext of hurling and playing football, crowds gathered, bands played, shouts were heard and fights broke out, confirming Catholic strength and highlighting residential disaffection. Protestants feared the worst, barricading their houses on fair days and remaining indoors. United Irishmen and Orangemen took to using these outings to start airing grievances, which always led to fights.

Thomas, son of Christopher Carey and brother of William, Matthew and James, owned a newspaper in Dublin. He was sympathetic to the cause of a united free Ireland, printing stories about absentee property owners and the terrible conditions rural folk were living in. These articles produced attacks from the establishment, which accused him of printing seditious stories. Thomas was tried at the Kings Bench and acquitted, but the ruling body continued to hound him and forced his printing business to close down.

The whole family were involved in the printing trade as either reporters or tradesmen. Matthew Carey (1785-1824) was internationally known as a publisher. Born in Dublin 1760, he was indentured to serve an apprenticeship as a letterpress printer, having to make up the sticks of type to be clamped into the forme. Later, befriended by Benjamin Franklin, he emigrated to America, where he married a Miss Flavahan, devoting all his energies to the publication of the Douay version of the Bible, founding the first American Sunday School Society and becoming one of America's greatest publishers.

Dublin, by the turn of the century, was the second biggest city in the British Isles. The most industrious and wealthy areas of Ireland were those closest to the English mainland, and in the middle of that coastline was Dublin, the seat of power, the legal centre and administrative capital. Its population contained the greatest number of professionals, guildsmen, artisans, journeymen and apprentices. This power gives a reason why Dublin was the centre of such unrest and revolution. The final straw was the drought of 1781. To provide freight and individual transportation a marvellous engineering scheme was put into place: the construction of a great canal and a series of locks to join Dublin to the River Shannon. This feat opened up the interior and controlled water distribution to the central plains, eliminating the fear of future droughts. Ireland was now an independent country but sharing a common monarch. In reality, many ties were there to prevent true self-government, which was never workable.

In 1790, an Act of Union saw London replace Dublin as the centre of political power for the Irish. Thomas Kearey was born the following year. 1791 was also the year when United Irishmen formed and Dublin barrister Theobald Wolfe Tone (1763-1798) published 'Argument on Behalf of the Catholics of Ireland', which brought about the emancipation of Ireland's Catholics ('The Story of Ireland', by Neil Hegarty).

By 1797, The United Irishmen were a powerful force in Leinster and plans were made for a general uprising. Oaths were taken and promises made to ensure a committed gathering, including tradespeople, shopkeepers and many of the middle class. The Orange Order objected and mass atrocities were perpetuated. Kilkeary Parish was reported by Ireland's Ordnance Survey as lying to the north of Co Tipperary between Nenagh, Cloghjordan, and Templemore, bounded to the east by Clonlisk in Kings. St. Ciardha's Church (Cill Cheire – Church of Keary) lay near the centre of the Barony of Upper Ormond, one and a half miles south-east of Toomevara. Kilkeary was one of the fourteen parishes in the barony.

In 1818, although there were a number of the family who used the Keary spelling, this was the first time that 'ey' was used in Ireland (Kearey), as recorded by Patrick and Mary [née Lonergan]. Unfortunately, it did not last long; they removed the 'e' five years later. After the passing of a few more years Carey (with or without the 'e'), Carew and Keary seemed to be an almost interchangeable choice by family members recorded in the Powerstown RC register. By the 1850s, Griffith's Primary Valuation gives 68 Kear[e]y households in all of Ireland.

Powerstown lies in the civil parish of Kilgrant in the barony of Iffa and Offa East, between Clonmel and the village of Kilsheelan.

It is difficult, from this distance, to comprehend the importance the spelling makes to the use of one's name. However, records prove that it does, prompted no doubt by strong reasons at the time. Even today, some family members feel free to use the Gaelic form whilst others use the anglicized version.

The amount of farmland in Ireland was now no longer enough to feed the expanding population. This applied in almost all regions, not just in the richer, more industrial sectors with the greatest labour forces. The problems stemmed from the way land was controlled, by rents and tithes. Tenure was restricted so that farmers budgeted and planned for short-term gain. This did not work well for the economic rotation of crops, the construction of land drainage ditches, the removal of stone from the fields or the latest views on animal husbandry; the use of better soil management to increase fertility was much talked about. The landowners, property owners and absentee property agents employed agents to collect the rents, which were transferred to England, the money making its way to English boroughs and the aristocracy. It was a case of negligence, ignorance, and lack of care on the part of local and national governments, in both England and Ireland. The potato blight finished off what the poor economy had started.

Many Irishmen and women in the middle of the nineteenth century lived close to where they were born, and were said never to leave their villages. Records disprove that assumption.

Reality dictates that this would be impossible. This was the age of large families. A large percentage of young people not long out of school would have to travel far to find work, and be trained for it. The local jobs market could not sustain such large numbers and houses were in short supply. By 1851, over fifty per cent of the population were living more than two miles from their birthplaces. The advent of the bicycle made travelling to work easier and the coming of the railways added to the distance travelled. It was the growth of towns and cities which drew the migrant workforce. It was not just the need to earn money or to find housing that made people move; it was exciting and enticing for the young, and the job options more varied.

The O'Ciardha family had lost much in the confiscations over the generations, keeping the less productive high lands as insurance – somewhere they could retreat to when times were hard. Irish politicians blamed the depressed state of the economy on England's restrictions of Irish trade. The poverty of the rural economy they blamed on those who maintained the pasturage instead of promoting the growing of seed crops and potatoes. In 1886 Gladstone's Liberal Party, with Irish support, brought a Home Rule bill before the Commons. Charles Stewart Parnell was the supporting Irish nationalist politician Leader of the Home Rule League in 1880 who died of heart failure at Brighton on 6th October 1891.

O'Hart's Irish Pedigrees of 1887, pp499, gives the 'Keary' family as MacCeachraigh of Galway, as distinct from Carey. (Mac, Mc and M mean the same as O – son of.) Keating's history gives the family as being numerous in Mayo and Sligo and states: 'there are other anglicized forms of the Gaelic name: the extinct Mac Fhiachra or Mac Fhearadhaigh, formally both of Tyrone and Galway, the synonym of Kerin (O'Ceirin or O'Ciarain) in Mayo and Cork. The English form of Mac Giolla Céire (Giolla means boy) further corrupted in Carr – (O'Carra and Mac Giolla Chathair) in Galway and Donegal and Mac Chathair in Co. Donegal. Keary and Carey are more likely to be found in Cork, Kerry and Tipperary'.

It would seem that it was mainly immigrants to America, England and the British Empire, at the turn of the eighteenth century, who used Keary/Kearey, the more anglicized form. Those worldwide who use the Carey form are however, more numerous. Dublin was a setting-off point for the immigrants, mostly to land at Liverpool. From there, a regular coach service to London and other major cities took the migrant to where there was work. If London-bound then it was to Westminster, and, as likely as not 'The Rookeries' (Little Ireland), where cheap lodging was to be found, perhaps with relatives.

My great-great-grandfather Thomas Kearey (1791-1860) arrived at the Liverpool dockside in 1816, with his bag of tools over his shoulder, ready to start a new life. He was born in Dublin city (COI) Ireland, (Archdiocese of Dublin, Baptisms, Nov. 1791 to Dec. 1791), baptised in St. Paul's Parish Church, Dublin, later that same year. His parents were James and Mary Keary, recorded DU-CI-BA-172933, Filename d-273-1-4-112. His 1841 and 1851 census forms and 20th March 1860 death certificate register Thomas as a baggage worker, and a gold and silver smelter and refiner. Three years later, in 17th October 1819, Thomas married Ester Pepler of Great Stanmore by banns (marriage by banns was a legal requirement; it was an announcement of a couple's intention to marry in church made on at least three Sundays in the three months preceding the wedding) in Saint Anne's Church, Soho, Westminster, the service conducted by the curate, Edward Bowman.

This was the age of The Great Reform Act of 1830, modernising the parliamentary system of England. Seven years later, Queen Victoria came to the throne. A further seven years later, Ireland suffered the Great Hunger, a famine that starved a million people to death.

Thomas and Ester were eventually to live in 20, North Row, Bromley. However, where Thomas lived in those years prior to meeting Ester, after his marriage, and before having children, is a mystery to be solved. It is now up to Timeline Genealogy Ireland to research, starting by delving into Charles James Jackson's English Goldsmiths London 1921, 2nd Ed, checking the Roll of Dublin Goldsmiths, with dates of admission and parentage (NLI GO665).

When Thomas marched down the gangplank, excited by the challenges that lay ahead, he sought passage to London by coach, relying on his skills as a worker in metal to find work – perhaps start a business – for Dublin's silversmiths and goldsmiths were recognised as highly skilled artisans. These skills, working with precious metals, could be carried over to working with tin and lead – metals more closely allied to the home – servicing water-tanks, pipes, buckets, cauldrons, washing and cooking pots and all other metal containers used in the home. Not only was he skilful shaping metal, he also had knowledge of joinery and the manufacture of carts.

Thomas married Ester Pepler (born Collins) in 1819. Her father, Edward Pepler, born 1767 in Great Stanmore, Middlesex, died in 1843. Thomas and Ester started a family one year later, in 1820, giving birth to a son, also named Thomas. His siblings William, Mary, Hester, Charlotte, Elizabeth and Emma made up the rest of the family.

That child was my great-great-grandfather (1821-1867) of St. Giles, Middlesex. He described himself as a whitesmith, which today maybe better described as a tinsmith, and as a smelter – an extractor of metal from ore. The O'Ciardha clan originally occupied the hills and lowlands on the east side of Lough Derg. The ore washed down from those hills would have been a combination of any number of metals. It would not be surprising to find local people adept at smelting that ore and either coating hammered-out sheets of metal with tin or combining tin and copper to make bronze or smelting lead and tin to make pewter. The smelter of any one ore would be knowledgeable enough to work with any number of base or precious metals. Tin wares were produced in London in the early 1600s, and producers became incorporated by 1670.

The skills of a whitesmith were more concerned with cutting, shaping and hammering out sheet metal, making joints and seams by using a mixture of lead and tin to make solder to give a watertight joint. Thomas may have worked in silver, making jewellery. However, it was highly unlikely that Thomas would have been working with this expensive metal. He would have been devoting all his energies to working with lead and tin in a household environment, making and repairing pipes and pans, pots and utensils for a working population.

In 1841 he married Hannah Raybould, who was born in 1822 in Fulham, her father a whitesmith. Thomas and Hannah had nine children, and again the first son was given the name of Thomas.

Dublin in the 1800s

Thomas Henry Kearey (1842-1900), my great-grandfather, was a highly trained blacksmith mainly engaged in manufacturing carriage wheel-rims.

He married Mary Ann Chuter, and his brother Alfred, my grandfather (1854-1917), a house painter and decorator, married Martha Sutton in 1878. They had eleven children. The first son was named Thomas Henry (1861-1882), his brother Albert (1889-1971) was my father, Albert Edward Kearey. https://www.albertkearey.co.uk/book/

Acknowledgements

Southern Irish History

It is important again to stress that details of names, places and time are impossible to confirm. Not only does the language change but the spelling within that language varies. Family groups within a tribe split into clans, and clans into septs. Kings are described as lords, and lords as kings. However, that should not present a problem. It is not a question of trying to change history or give credence but present a picture of where the Ciardha fit into early Christian Irish country life.

History of the Ely O'Carroll printed by Boethius Press. Additional Material: Robert Books Limited, 1982, in Toomevara Parish.

The Last Lords of Ormond, *The Curse of Cromwell*, by Dermot F. Gleeson. Revised New Edition by Donal A. Murphy. Published by Relay.

The Ordnance Survey Name Books, which describes parish boundaries, the origin of place names, and the monuments of historical value – reference Kilkeary.

The Civil Survey of 1654-656, Vol. II, carried out at the time of the Cromwellian confiscations.

Kept close by, throughout all my studies of ancient Ireland, have been:

The Course of Irish History by Moody & Martin (4th Edition); *A History of Ireland* by Mike Cronin; *The Great Hunger* by Cecil Woodham-Smith; and *The Age of Arthur* by John Morris, *The Book of Kells* by Bernard Meehan; I am grateful for their research and dedication. I am particularly thankful for the help of Tipperary Library and Library of Ireland.

Kilkeary is situated in Upper Ormond, four miles from Nenagh. It contains 2,524 statute acres, and in 1837 there were 662 inhabitants. The name is recorded by Aengus as Cill Cheri, and written "Ciar Ingen Duibhrea, Saint Ciar, the daughter of Duibhrea, the church of Saint Kera or Cera, and situated in the ancient Muscraidhe Thire – the two Ormonds.

The Last Lords of Ormond, The Curse of Cromwell, by Dermot F. Gleeson. New Edition with revisions by Donal A. Murphy. Published by Relay.

Their land fractions, allotted after 1657, were lost again in the Williamite wars, to the 'Discoverers'. In Ormond some of the foremost of the Old Irish gentry took refuge in the remote and almost inaccessible valley of Glenculloo between the Slieve Felim hills, from which their descendants to this day carry their dead to their ancestral graveyards in Ballinaclogh and Kilkeary. There are seven further references to Kilkeary in this publication.

The Ordnance Survey Name Books, which describes parish boundaries, the origin of place names and the monuments of historical value found in them, refer to Kilkeary.

In the Civil Survey of 1654-1656, Vol. II, carried out at the time of the Cromwellian confiscations, Kilkeary is mentioned thus:

The Parish of Kylkeary, 1640. The Meares and Bounds of the sayd Parish at large sett forth with the severall Townships and parcells of land therein conteyned. And the Tythes of ye sd Parish of 120 Acres made up from 80 Arable, 10 meddow and 20 pasture. It also contains 10 Acres of bog. The Proprietors names given as Daniell mc Henry Kenedy of Lisheen and John Fyhola of Ballynamona.

During a personal visit to the area I found that Toomevara Parish have Kilkeary as part of their area of control, the state school and graveyard being added in 2009. Nenagh Co. Tipperary Council Highways are responsible for the upkeep of the graveyard and environs. Greenanstown House is the seat of Count D'Alton.

The meaning of Kil or Cill before the place-name is given in Collins' Irish Dictionary as nf2 church, graveyard, cemetery using the example of cill agus tuath, Church and State. There is no K in the Gaeilge language, which directs us to the Latinized Cheire or Ciar pronunciation and their spelling as Ceary, Keary, or in places Kearey (Therefore Church of Keary is the correct English translation for Kilkeary). Once again resorting to Collins Gaeilge dictionary, 'Ciar' (gsm céir, gst, compar céire) adj (hair) means dark: (complexion) dark, swarthy, Gk Ierne.

OCelt. Human population movement (Native) of Ireland from the Spanish Peninsula.

A king of Ulster was named Ciar. After being banished from the court of Cruochan, he sought refuge in west Munster. There he gained the territory of the first branch of the Carraige Tribe he called Luachre in County Kerry. *Taken from* Irish Kings and High Kings, *p160, 236, and 247. By France John Byrne, third Edition, Dublin 2001.*

Investigations into family history have revealed that Kearey, or rather Keary or Ceary, translates, by the use of Gælic/Irish, from Ó Ciardha and is closely related to the Cahill family of Connaught.

From the late ninth century, surnames were not passed down in Ireland but were patronymic – based on the father's name and added after the first name, therefore Thomas Ó Ceary = Thomas the son of Ceary. Later, in the 12th century, when the Normans ruled and lived in Ireland, they soon learned the language and this use of names. The English government passed a law that required all Englishmen in Ireland to have an English name and to speak English. Today the names beginning with O', stemming from Ó, means 'the grandson of, or descendant of.

Around the year 1387 the O'Clery were traditional poets. When writing Gaelic or Irish the Ó has the accent above the O, while when writing English the prefix is after, thus O'.

From early times the first-born son of the family was called Thomas. Thomas O'Ciardha, brother of Desmond O'Ciardha of Offaly, was called Thomas Baintreabhachd (or 'Thomas the Widower'), and was the ancestor of "Keary," of Fore, County

Meath. This Thomas lived on the Hill commanding a view of the famous Abbey, founded at Fore by St. Fechin, and was killed in the burning of the Abbey by the Cromwellians, A.D.1654.

Commencing with the said Thomas, the following is the pedigree of this family:

1. Thomas had three sons, Thomas, Patrick, and James, three of whom sought refuge, and found it, with Hugh O'Byrne, of Dublin, one of the Confederate Catholics; Patrick and James died unmarried. The eldest son, Thomas, married Mary O'Byrne, niece of the above-named Hugh, and had three sons, Thomas, Patrick, and Hugh. Both Patrick and Hugh went to Spain where Hugh married Margaret, daughter of Dermot O'Brien of Naas, having five children: Dermot, Thomas, Patrick, John, and Mary. Patrick entered Spanish service. John was married in 1745 to Mary, daughter of Owen M'Kewen of Clontarf and Swords, and had one son, Thomas, b1747, and a daughter, Ellen, b1749, who was married in 1780 to Hugh O'Moore of the O'Moores of Longford. Thomas married Julia, daughter of Roderick Murphy of Castledermot, in 1815, having four children, Thomas, John, Patrick and Michael.

Daniel O'Ciardha (or O'Cary), a nephew of Thomas and Julia, having conformed to the Protestant religion, called together the remnant of his family and, in order to distinguish themselves from the said Daniel, they solemnly pledged to assume thereafter the name of Keary, and to abandon the prefix and the 'Carey' form of the name.

Thomas married Mary, daughter of John Keogh of Castlepollard, in 1815; he was the first to omit the prefix O' from the family name, then O'Cary, and assumed the name Keary. This Thomas died in Dublin in 1836 and was buried in the churchyard of Artane, where his tomb still lies. Thomas and Mary had five children: Patrick, John, Michael (d. Liverpool 1870), Bridget and Mary. Patrick married Anne, youngest daughter of James Butler of Fairview, Ballybough, Dublin, and died in 1884. They had ten children: Thomas, Frances, Michael, James, John, Peter, Joseph, Matthew, Patrick and Mary-Anne.

Patrick J. Keary (Cahill), son of Patrick (ninth son of Patrick and Anne) of Colville Terrace, Ballybough Road, and of Wellington Quay, Dublin, married Elizabeth, only daughter of Patrick Cahill, in 1875. They had four children: William-Laurence Cahill Keary, b1877, John-Frances, b1887, Mary-E., and Christina.

Sources

History of the Ely O'Carroll. Printed by Boethius Press. Additional Material: Robert Books Limited, 1982, in Toomevara Parish.

The Last Lords of Ormond, The Curse of Cromwell, by Dermot F. Gleeson. New edition with revisions by Donal A. Murphy. Published by Relay.

The Ordnance Survey Name Books, which describe parish boundaries, the origin of place names and the monuments of historical value. Found in them are references to Kilkeary.

Dioceses of Killaloe and Kilfenora. Page 37, No. 3, Kilkeary, Reet, Entire. Titled April 7th 1808, being one fourth of the deanery.

Typographical Dictionary of Ireland by Samuel Lewis. Volume 2. Published by S. Lewis and Co. Aldersgate Street, London.

Kilkeary is a Parish in the Barony of Upper Ormond, County of Tipperary and Province of Munster, four miles (south-east) from Nenagh on the road to Cashel, and containing 662 inhabitants, it comprises 2,524 statute acres: the land is generally good and mostly under tillage. Greenanstown House is the seat of Count D'Alton, the parish is in the diocese of Killaloe and is a rectory forming part of the union of Ballynaclough and corps of the Deanery of Killaloe: the tithes amount to £120. About 70 children are educated in a private school. (Recorded in 1837, page 75, Vol 2.)

The parish system in Ireland began in 700 and AD 1300. By the 12th century a system based on the local community – the tuath, perhaps a tuath-church system, a mixture of rectories and vicarages incorporating both secular and ecclesiastical concerns, was established.

> The Civil Survey of 1654-1656, Vol. II was carried out at the time of the Cromwellian confiscations.
>
> *Early Irish Saints* by John J. O' Riordàin CSsR.
>
> Wikipedia: Cathal Crobhdearg Ua Conchobair.
>
> Kilkenny Archaeological Society 1855, *The Life and Times of Cathal.*
>
> Annals of the Four Masters: M1205.10. Teige, the son of Cathal Crovderg Family Tree.
>
> Library of Ireland, History Cahill family genealogy - Irish Pedigrees.
>
> Adomnàn of Iona, *Life of St Columba*, Translated by Richard Sharpe. Penguin Classic 1995.
>
> Kept close by, throughout all my studies of ancient Ireland, was *The Origins of the Irish* by J. P. Mallory.
>
> *The Course of Irish, A Guide to Tracing your Dublin*

Ancestors, by James G. Ryan. Flyleaf Press 1988.

History by Moody & Martin (fourth edition); *A History of Ireland,* by Mike Cronin; John, Canon O'Hanlon (1821-1905); *The Great Hunger* by Cecil Woodham-Smith; *The Age of Arthur* by John Morris; and *Omnium Sanctorum Hibernia*, (2012-2015) by Saint Cera (Ciar) of Kilkeary.

I am grateful for the research and dedication of the above. I am particularly thankful for the help of Tipperary Library, whose staff have always been most generous, and to Michael Keary and his abundant studies. I have read the autobiography of Peig, written at the time of my birth, to get a feel for the Gaelic/Irish speaker's life in outposts of Ireland's south-western countryside where the Ciariaidhe, particularly the O'Ciardha, made for, to escape clan and foreign warfare.

It would be remiss not to mention John O'Hart, *Irish Pedigrees* or *The Origin and Stem of the Irish Nation*, fifth edition, in two volumes. Baltimore: Genealogical Publishing Co. 1976. Print. (ISBN 0-8063-0737-4) first printed in Dublin 1880. (John O'Hart has made in the past a number of genealogical mistakes. I have removed two family trees which have been based upon O'Hart's writings. Alpha Editions 2019, or the 'Four Masters', principally collected by the monk St. Francis, Michael O'Clery, during the period 1616-1682, and the work of Sir J. Bernard Burke, C.B., LL.D., Ulster King of Arms.

It would appear that ''Ciar' was the ancestor of the people named 'Ciariaidhe' after whom the O'Conor ('Kerry') sept was the leading family of the Irian race, taking the name of one of their great chiefs of the eleventh century from both Con and Ciar, their great ancestor, to form the name of Conor (Conior), page 228, County Kerry. *The Stem* Part II, The House of Ir, pages 86 and 92. The House of Heremon, page 202, gives Carey (Keary) as a leading family. *The Four Masters* mentioned O'Carey, chiefs of Cairbre 'Carbery' (page 282). The index converts the 'C' into 'K' covering Keary, Ceary and Kieran (pages 896 and 897). Working with Herald Donal Burke to form the clan was most rewarding researching the history and choosing the armorial ensigns the culmination of the task.

The task of looking back in time, prior to Thomas (1791-1860) and perhaps before his parents, James and Mary, has been given to Timeline Genealogy Ireland.

https://www.keareyclan.org/
https://www.openwindowslearning.co.uk/

The statement or position beneath, sent by the Chief Herald of Ireland (received 18th May 2022) about the family motto 'Truth be told' being added to the final document:

To all to whom these Presents shall come I, Colette O'Flaherty, Chief Herald of Ireland, send Greeting.

Whereas petition hath been made unto me by Terence Arthur Kearey of Petworth, West Sussex, England, born at North Harrow, Middlesex, the son of Albert Edward Kearey of North Harrow, Middlesex, the grandson of Alfred Kearey of Salem Gardens in the same country, the great grandson of Thomas Kearey of Sutton Street, Kensington in the same country, the great, great grandson of Thomas Kearey of North Row, Kensington in the same country, who was born in Ireland, setting forth that he is desirous that certain Armorial Ensigns may be duly marshalled and assigned by lawful authority unto him such as without injury or prejudice to any other he may forever bear and advance and praying I would grant and assign unto him and his descendants such Armorial Ensigns as aforesaid and that the Armorial Ensigns so granted and assigned may be duly ratified and recorded in the Office of the Chief herald of Ireland to the end that the Officers of Arms there and all others upon occasion may take notice and have Knowledge thereof.

Now I, the said Chief Herald of Ireland, having taken this matter into consideration am pleased to comply with the said petition and by virtue of the power vested in me in that behalf do by these Presents grant and assign until the said Terence Arthur Kearey the Arms following, that is to say, per fess rayonné Sable and Or on a chief Argent four crosses couped of the first and on a wreath of colours the Crest: a demi-panther incensed rampant guardant Argent semée of torteaux, hurts and pommes alternately, flames issuant from the mouth and ears holding in each paw a blacksmith's hammer Proper on a helmet mantled Gules doubled Argent the whole depicted in the margin hereof with the motto 'Truth be Told'. To have and to hold the said Arms unto the said Terence Arthur Kearey and to his descendants forever and the same to bear, use, shew, set forth and advance in shield or banner or otherwise each observing and using their due and proper differences according to the Laws of Arms and the practice of this Office and without the let, hindrance, molestation, interruption, controlment or challenge of any manner of person or persons whatsoever, excepting always the Author and authority of this Office.

An Irish connection; "From O'Ciardha to Keary'

Keary, of Fore, County Westmeath

This family is believed to be a branch of the Cahill family of Connaught, which derived its name from Cathal, who in No.102 of the Cahill of Connaught pedigree; was in Irish known as O'Ciardha (ciar in Irish for a dark-grey colour), anglicized O'Cearry, O'Carry, O'Carrie, Carry, Carey, and Keary etc.

Thomas O'Ciardha, brother of Dermod O'Ciardha of Offaley, called Thomas Baintreabhachd (or Thomas the Widower), wass the ancestor of "Keary" of Fore, county Meath. This Thomas lived on the Hill commanding a view of the famous Abbey founded at Fore by St.Fechin; and was killed at the burning of the Abbey by the Cromwellians, A.D.1654.

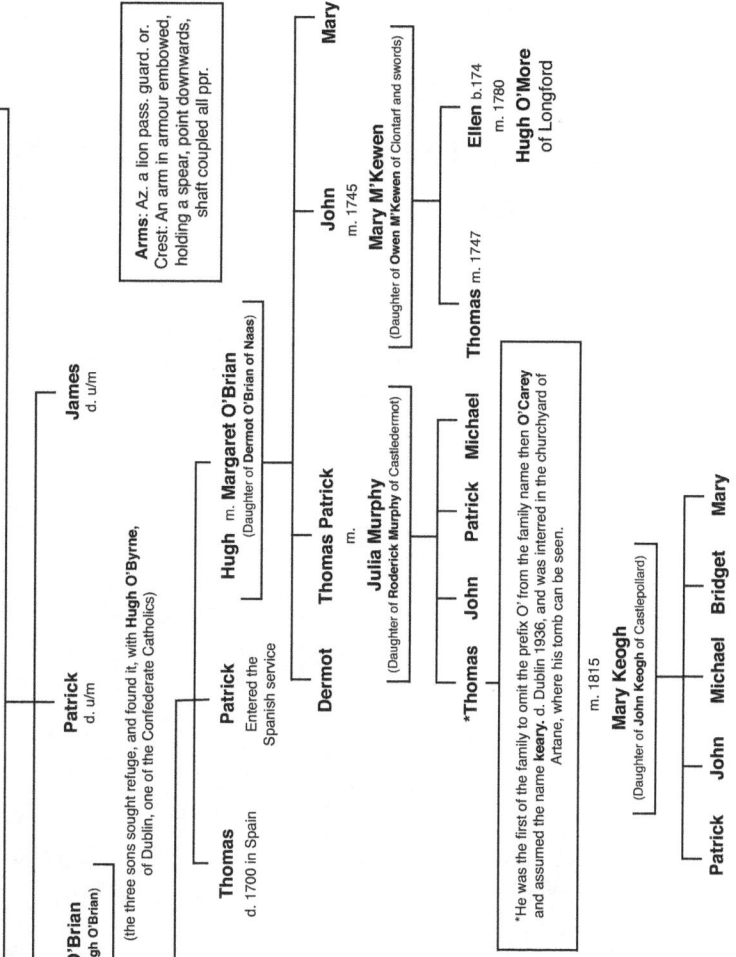

Arms: Az. a lion pass. guard. or. Crest: An arm in armour embowed, holding a spear, point downwards, shaft coupled all ppr.

Thomas m. **Mary O'Brian**
(Niece of **Hugh O'Brian**)

Patrick d. u/m

James d. u/m

(the three sons sought refuge, and found it, with **Hugh O'Byrne**, of Dublin, one of the Confederate Catholics).

Patrick
Entered the Spanish service

Thomas
d. 1700 in Spain

Hugh m. **Margaret O'Brian**
(Daughter of **Dermot O'Brian of Naas**)

Dermot   **Thomas Patrick**
m.
Julia Murphy
(Daughter of **Roderick Murphy** of Castledermot)

*Thomas   John   Patrick   Michael

*He was the first of the family to omit the prefix O' from the family name then O'**Carey** and assumed the name **keary.** d. Dublin 1936, and was interred in the churchyard of Artane, where his tomb can be seen.

John   **Mary**
m. 1745
Mary M°Kewen
(Daughter of **Owen M°Kewen** of Clontarf and swords)

Thomas m. 1747

Ellen b.174
m. 1780
Hugh O'More
of Longford

m. 1815
Mary Keogh
(Daughter of **John Keogh** of Castlepollard)

Patrick   John   Michael   Bridget   Mary

***Daniel O'Ciardha (or O'Cary).** A nephew of this **Thomas**, having conformed to the Protestant religion, caused **Thomas** to call together the remnant of his family; and in order to distinguish themselves from the said Daniel, they solemnly pledged to assume thereafter the name Keary, to abandon the prefix O'. and the "Carey" form of spelling the name.

IRELAND.

www.ingramcontent.com/pod-product-compliance
Lightning Source LLC
Chambersburg PA
CBHW032138040426
42449CB00005B/298